THE GREAT TRAIN ROBBERY

THE GREAT

THE BOBBS-MERRILL COMPANY, INC. A SUBSIDIARY OF HOWARD W. SAMS

JOHN

GOSLING

AND

DENNIS

CRAIG

TRAIN ROBBERY

CO., INC. PUBLISHERS · INDIANAPOLIS · KANSAS CITY · NEW YORK

Copyright © 1964, 1965 by John Gosling and Dennis Craig
Library of Congress catalog card number 65-16294

Printed in the United States of America

CONTENTS

A note for the reader

The reader will remember that the rate
of exchange varies from day to day.
On August 8, 1963, £1 was worth slightly
more than $2.80. For the reader's convenience,
the American equivalent of the British
figure is bracketed throughout the book.

PREFACE

At 3 o'clock on the morning of Thursday, August 8, 1963, the Royal Mail train from Glasgow to London was roaring through the lush countryside of Buckinghamshire at eighty miles an hour. During the next hectic twenty-eight minutes—less time than it takes to chain-smoke three cigarettes—the train was stopped, the engine and two front coaches hijacked, the driver and fireman overpowered and handcuffed; a team of five Post Office sorters lay huddled together on the floor of the front coach, completely subdued.

ix

And the mail train's bumper cargo of £2,600,000 [$7,282,600 in dollars at the rate of exchange on that day] in banknotes was stolen and loaded aboard waiting motor trucks.

It had been a robbery of military precision on an unprecedented scale. The British taxpayer received the news that he had been relieved of more than £2½ [$7¼] million of his own money with bemused delight. He was still licking his wounds from a succession of scandals which rocked the nation; the summer of 1963 was proving the coldest and wettest in living memory after the most severe winter on record.

The cool daring of the raid and the enormous sum of money involved was like a tonic, a badly-needed fillip to offset the misery of a sunless summer. Only the most serious-minded railed against the fact that in the end it would be the public's money that made good the loss. In an age of free vouchers, trading stamps and dreams of quick riches via the football pools there were chuckles in place of condemnation and the toast in pubs and clubs throughout the land was "the best of British luck to them."

While bank shares slumped on the London Stock Exchange—National Provincial Bank shares shed 1s. 1½ d. [$.15⅙] overnight—all sorts of weird and irrelevant calculations were being made. It was worked out that the stolen money was sufficient to pay for all the beer consumed in Great Britain in twenty-four hours. If the robbers were men of social conscience they could build housing for 850 families, or, if they wanted to be mercenary, they could make a fair-sized City takeover bid. Robert Head, the *Daily Mirror's* enterprising financial editor, pointed out that the loot was £100,000 [$280,100] more than Unilever paid when they bought the firm that manufactured and marketed Domestos and Squezy washing-up liquid.

Echoes of praise from across the Atlantic quickened the pulse of British pride. The Empire might have been lost and an independent nuclear deterrent turn out to be a mere politician's pipe-dream, but the British underworld could at least teach Chicago gangsters something about organized crime.

The New York *Herald Tribune*, which published the story on its front page under the six-column headline, "History's Greatest Robbery—there'll always be an England," commented: "Although train robbery is likely to be associated with America's wild west, this fell deed has a peculiarly British quality.

"Perhaps because of a long tradition of highly literate writers on sophisticated crime, British criminals tend to avoid the blood-and-thunder style of the James boys and do their work with exceptional finesse."

The New York Times, writing tongue-in-cheek, found it a fitting occasion to jeer at the techniques of American hoodlums.

"How pallid our own crime syndicates are made to

look, how wanting in imagination," the newspaper commented. "After all, we hold the copyright on train robbery. We even put them on film half-a-century ago in
the first movie with a fully-developed plot, 'The Great
Train Robbery,' yet now the best we can say about this
updating of Jesse James is that we supplied the cultural
inspiration. The know-how is distinctly British. Or were
some enterprising members of the American underworld
there in a patriotic effort to help even out our balance of
international payments?"

Not for one moment was America's most responsible
newspaper going to take this British crime coup seriously.
It expressed the hope that "the imperturbable James
Bond" had been put on the case and added: "Undoubtedly Goldfinger or Dr. No is behind this incredibly
efficient bit of larceny."

The British Press's editorial comment was generally
devoted to pointing out how well organized crime had
become and how inadequate were the precautions. But
for the train robbers themselves there were distinct un-
dertones of admiration. The mass-circulation *Daily
Express* alone felt it had a duty to discourage such at-
titudes and delivered this admonitory rap in a leader
under the melodramatic heading "Brutal Plot."

"There should be no disposition to look on the train
robbers as master minds, or to admire their 'genius' for
large-scale crime. For what happened at Sears Cross-

ing? A gang of armed bandits held up unarmed railmen and GPO workers.

"They made a gigantic haul through simple criminal brutality. Their plot depended on terrorizing train drivers into silence. What is daring or brilliant about that?

"The real organizing ability comes from those whose job it is to track down criminals—the police."

But the police were getting nowhere and only the offer of the greatest reward in history—£260,000 [$728,-260] for detection of the thieves and recovery of the money—jerked the public of Britain into any sort of action against the train robbers. Posses of amateur sleuths combed the countryside of Buckinghamshire and the surrounding counties in search of buried treasure. In and around London professional informers worked overtime in haunts of the underworld and inundated the two firms of loss adjustors—Hart and Company, and Topliss and Harding—with information. Most of it proved valueless.

At the time of writing seven men have been found guilty of stopping the train and robbing it. Seven others, including three women, are charged with receiving sums of money alleged to be part of the robbery. Some £280,000 [$784,280], representing little more than one-tenth of the haul, has been recovered.

What of the other £2,300,000 [$6,442,300] still missing?

After months of painstaking private investigation ex-Detective-Superintendent John Gosling, the co-author of this book and former head of the now legendary Ghost Squad, is convinced that the bulk of the money will never be recovered nor even traced, and that no matter which members of the gang are captured and convicted, the man who master-minded the plot will escape justice.

Every investigator on the case of the Great Train Robbery has his own theory about who did it and how it was planned. The more conventional police officers reject the possibility of a master-mind whose identity remains unknown to most of the gang. To them following such a line would be as profitable as chasing a rainbow. But in fact this is exactly what they should be doing—for Johnnie Rainbow was the code-name of the man who conceived, planned and brilliantly directed this biggest theft in history.

HOW THE JOB
WAS DONE

1

The man who masterminded the world's greatest train
robbery was never in any doubt about his target. The
train which pulled out of Platform 11 at Glasgow Central
Station shortly before 7 p.m. on August 7, 1963, was, as
on every Wednesday following August Bank Holiday
Monday, carrying the year's biggest consignment of
English banknotes.

1

These had been spent by the tens of thousands of English tourists who had made their annual sortie across the border for three or four bracing days in Scotland away from it all. Within two days of the end of the holiday most of the money had, as usual, been banked and parceled up for return to England. Scotland prints its own banknotes so that English notes, although accepted as currency, are not paid out by banks in Scotland but are transferred daily to their London offices for redistribution.

The money, on this occasion amounting to more than £2-million [$5,602,000], was loaded with other mail aboard the traveling post office which for many years had left Glasgow at the same time on every week night.

At exactly 6:50 p.m. some seventy Post Office sorters went through the routine of locking themselves in the twelve coaches that comprised the train. Five of the men sealed themselves in the high-value coach, traditionally placed second from the engine.

The departure of the train on its 401–mile journey to London's Euston Station and the fact that some 100 bags of notes—easily identifiable to anyone familiar with the system of mailbag markings—were put aboard at Glasgow was undoubtedly telephoned to the mastermind in London. There was no real secrecy or security about this routine nightly procedure which could not be bought for the price of a platform ticket.

As the train sped southwards, pulled by one of the

Railway's latest experimental engines, a 1B 2,000-horse-power diesel, the bags of notes and other valuable mail were being separated from the ordinary mail in the rear coaches and passed forward to the men in the high-value coach. There it was sorted and then stacked in padlocked wooden cupboards ranged along the side.

There were so many bags stuffed full of £5 [$14.00] and £1 [$2.80] notes that even without the additional bags picked up en route at Carlisle, Crewe and Rugby, the lockers were filled. Sixty bags had to be piled on the floor, making it difficult for the sorters to walk down the narrow corridor without tripping over.

The men commented on the unusually large amount they were handling, but no-one had the slightest worry even though the self-locking anti-bandit coaches that they would normally have traveled in were in the repair shops. In 125 years of transporting money via the traveling post office there had never been an attempt to rob it. They were going at seventy miles an hour, they were dead on time, and everything was proceeding as usual.

But down the line, thirty-nine miles from London between Sears Crossing and Cheddington, there was feverish activity. Months of careful planning and rehearsal were about to be put to the test. This was the night selected by the head of a gang of fifteen men to bring an end to more than a century of cozy Post Office history.

About 2 a.m. the members of the gang, who were dressed in overalls, drove in two Landrovers and a larger truck from their temporary headquarters at Leatherslade Farm, an isolated hillside house surrounded by meadows, which lay sixteen miles from Sears Crossing.

They parked their vehicles off the lonely road near Bridego Bridge, Cheddington. The moon was on the wane, but gave enough light for the men to go about their preliminary tasks without flashing torches. While one group isolated the neighborhood by cutting telephone wires, the gang's signals expert, who could also drive a train, walked 1,000 yards up the line and disconnected the approach signal. Next he blacked out the green signal for "Go" at Sears Crossing and by connecting two terminals to dry batteries, set it on red.

Before settling down to wait for the train each man was issued a signal flag. These, combined with their blue Railway-type overalls, would allay immediate suspicion when the driver and his mate, obeying the signal to halt, saw them on the line.

On the footplate of the powerful diesel the driver, fifty-seven-year-old Jack Mills, and fireman David Whitby, aged twenty-six, had just downed their last brew of tea. London was less than an hour away. Both men lived at Crewe and planned to spend the night in the Railway's comfortable hostel at Camden Town.

In the high-value coach chief sorter Frank Dewhurst, a taciturn, stocky forty-nine-year-old Londoner, was making a final inspection. All the money and registered

4

mail had by now been passed through from the back of the train and the job of sorting was almost completed.

When driver Mills saw the red signal, the thought that it might be anything out of the ordinary did not cross his mind. He reacted automatically, for such unscheduled stops are a normal factor in any railway system with heavy traffic. He brought the engine to a smooth halt and he and the fireman peered out on the dimly-lit track.

"There should be a telephone to the signal box just down there," said Mills, pointing off the track. "Phone through and ask them how long the delay's going to be."

Whitby jumped down and found the telephone where the driver had indicated. He tried it and realized at once that the line was dead. Then he saw that the wires had been neatly severed, and for the first time on that journey somebody sensed that all was not well. He shouted up to Mills, "Jack, the wires are cut!" and he started back toward the train.

At this moment two things happened simultaneously. A man with his features masked in a woolen balaclava appeared on the steps of Mills's cab. In his hand he carried a long stick wrapped in white cloth. The driver did not hesitate. In his own words: "I thought, 'I'm not giving in without a fight.' "

He leaped at the marauder and grappled with him. There was a short furious struggle and Mills, who had the advantage of the height of his footplate while the other man was on the step, was gaining the upper hand. He rained blows and kicks on his assailant, but as he was preparing a final great effort to throw the man down on the track he was coshed from behind by another raider. He collapsed on to his knees and was immediately battered on the head by both men. Astonishingly this sturdy middle-aged warrior of the footplate did not lose consciousness. His body, toughened by years of coalheaving as a young man on steam engines, refused to submit until he was helplessly groggy. He heard somebody say, "Don't look up or you'll get some more." Then he lay still.

In the meanwhile Whitby, making his way back to the footplate, suddenly saw, between the second and third coach, a man carrying regulation signal flags. He was relieved to see him; here was someone who could explain what was happening.

"What's up, mate?" he called.

The man with the flags walked toward him beckoning and said, "Come over here." It was not until they met face to face beside the first coach on the edge of the embankment that Whitby realized that the man he had taken to be a railwayman was wearing a balaclava mask. Before he could gather his senses the man gave him a hefty push and he toppled backwards down the bank. So carefully had the gang laid their plans that another bandit was waiting for him at the bottom of the slope. The second man grabbed him, put a hand over Whitby's mouth and brandished a cosh.

"If you shout, I'll kill you," he hissed.

There was no doubt in the young co-driver's mind that these men in masks were thugs and there seemed no point in resisting. In fact, he decided that for his own safety he had better co-operate to the fullest. Winded and terrified, he told his assailant, "All right, mate—I'm on your side."

The bandit gave him a hard look. There was obviously going to be no trouble from this quarter.

"Thanks," he said dryly.

Whitby was led back to the engine. Among the crowd of eight or nine masked men now in the cab he saw Mills on his knees, bleeding profusely.

Both men were dragged into the passage leading to the engine room.

Now the gang struck their only snag in the whole operation. In the brief time they had been in the cab their railways expert, who had expected to drive the engine, discovered it was a new type that he was unable to handle. There was a quick whispered discussion, and it was decided that they should press Mills into service. One of the gang came to the engine room and told the men holding the two prisoners, "We want the driver."

Mills was dragged back to the footplate.

"Keep your head down. Don't look up," they warned him. When he was in the chair he was ordered, "Look straight ahead. Don't turn around."

There was a wait. Although Mills and Whitby did not

realize at this stage what was happening the third coach and all behind it were being uncoupled from the second, the first and the engine. It was done so quietly and efficiently that there was no sound to arouse the suspicions of the sorters in any of the coaches.

The signal was given to pull away. Mills started the engine, now dragging only the first two coaches.

"When I say stop," said the man standing behind him, "you stop—or you'll get some more."

Mills drove the train slowly down the line for about a mile. Blood was filling his eyes; he was sick and dizzy after the terrific beating he had received. What would happen when the job was done? It was small reassurance when one of the gang who had the humanity to wipe the blood from his face warned him in a whisper, "For God's sake don't speak. There are some right bastards here. Keep quiet, for your own sake."

When they reached Bridego Bridge driver Mills was told to stop the train and he put the brakes on. Whitby was brought up to him and the two men were handcuffed together. They were made to get down from the engine and lie by the side of the rail. One man stood guard over them.

Experienced sorters on traveling Post Offices are so used to stops and work at such a pace that they rarely even notice whether the train is moving or not. The first intimation to the Post Office men that the train was being attacked came when a side window of the high-value coach was shattered.

"It's a raid!" one of the postmen shouted. Frank Dewhurst, the chief sorter, grabbed two of the mailbags and rushed to the window in a desperate but futile attempt to barricade the break. At the same time he shouted to his assistants to lock the gangway door. He knew the side doors were bolted.

From the outside he heard a man shout, "Some bastard's putting the bolts on. Get the guns."

The next moment he was confronted by a heavily-built masked man who had smashed his way in with an axe. The raider raised the weapon above his head. Dewhurst put his hand out to ward him off. Then he was hit several times from behind by others of the gang who were now streaming in. The unarmed Post Office men, faced with about fifteen raiders brandishing axes, coshes and crowbars, could do nothing. They were herded into a corner and told to lie on the floor. Someone nudged Dewhurst in the ribs with his boot.

"You all right?" said the man.

"Yes!" gasped Dewhurst.

"Right. Now listen. You lot stay here on the floor for half an hour after we've gone. We're leaving someone behind to make sure you don't move, and God help you if you do."

As he spoke the rest of the gang were already fever-

9

ishly engaged in passing out the bags of money which lay on the floor and smashing the padlocks on the wooden cupboards to get at the rest.

From outside Mills and Whitby, still lying next to the track, watched the gang form a human chain from the coach to the lorries parked under the bridge but out of their line of vision. The man guarding them was visibly elated at the sight. He turned to his two prisoners.

"I'll get your address when all this is over and send you a few quid," he said.

With his one free hand Whitby groped in his pockets and pulled out a packet of cigarettes. He lit one and tried to give it to Mills.

"I'll have one if you've got one to spare," said their guard in a tone of unexpected courtesy, and borrowed his lighter to light it.

In a few more minutes it was over. The driver and his mate, still handcuffed together, were bundled into the second coach with the five sorters, and again they were warned to stay on the floor for half an hour.

There was silence. None of the seven men in the coach moved as they listened to the sound of motors starting up.

Then the noise receded into the distance. Still they kept motionless. There was the possibility that anyone who put his head out might get shot.

After ten minutes Dewhurst got up. Cautiously he looked out, but he could see no-one. He climbed down, walked round the train, and, satisfied that no-one had been left to keep watch, went back to the coach and sent two of his men off to raise the alarm. They struck across country. About a mile from the bridge they came to Ridborough Farm and roused Mr. Cecil Rawding, the owner.

They gasped out their story to him and asked to use the telephone.

"I haven't one," he said. "The best I can do is lend you my bicycle. The nearest telephone's at Linslade, down the road."

While one of the men took the cycle and pedaled away to the village, Farmer Rawding told the other how he had recently seen strangers photographing the area with a ciné camera.

"And two days ago," he said, "my wife told me there had been a van parked under the bridge all night."

By the time the cyclist reached Linslade help had already arrived at the plundered train. Back down the line, Tom Miller, the guard, who had got out to investigate the long delay, discovered that the ten coaches at the rear had been uncoupled from the engine. When, in his turn, he found the telephone wires cut he hurried along the track in the direction taken by the engine.

In the meanwhile there had been growing concern at Cheddington Station at the delay in the mail train's arrival.

At about 3:30 a.m., just after the raiders had flung

the last bag into the trucks, the duty signalman at Ched-dington telephoned Leighton Buzzard to inquire if the train had passed through there. Told that it had gone through half an hour earlier he realized that the train must be stopped between the two points. A parcels train was sent along the line to search for it.

The search train, traveling slowly down the line, was stopped at the scene of the crime by one of the postmen flashing a torch and the seven victims of the raid were quickly transferred to it, Mills and Whitby still hand-cuffed together. They were not separated until they got to the Royal Buckinghamshire Hospital at Aylesbury where Mills was treated and put to bed.

The first astonished reports in the afternoon news-papers of August 8 announced that the gang "may have got away with a £1,000,000 haul"—the biggest in the history of Scotland Yard. A conference of all C.I.D. chiefs was hurriedly called.

The Postmaster-General, Mr. Reginald Bevins, cut short his holiday in Spain to fly to London where he faced a barrage of critical questions by reporters.

Mr. Bevins frankly admitted, "Clearly our security arrangements have been unsatisfactory and need exam-ining as quickly as possible. We cannot altogether rule out the possibility that the raid was an inside job."

But when asked, "Just how easy is it to rob a train?" he gave this extraordinary reply: "It is difficult. We have forty traveling Post Offices running between London and other parts of the country and this is the first time there has been a robbery from one in 125 years."

It seemed to those listening and to those who afterwards read this remark that it must be one of the easiest things in the world to rob a British mail train. The fact that this was the first robbery was more a reflection on the enterprise of past generations of criminals than on the difficulties placed in their way by Post Office security.

The loss in the present case, Mr. Bevins said, was about £1-million.

Two men, a detective-superintendent and a sergeant, were sent from Scotland Yard to help the Buckinghamshire police with their investigations—a fact which caused much angry comment among the senior detectives. They knew that they would eventually be called in to take over but, as so often happens, this would not be done until the trail was cold. Instead of being sent in by the dozen to comb the area it was the old story of "send two men" who could do little but examine the engine, coaches and track which yielded no worthwhile clues.

On August 9, some thirty-six hours after the raid, the banks released figures showing how much they had lost. These confirmed what most newspapers had claimed all along—that in spite of the Postmaster-General's estimate, the loss was nearer £3-million [$8,403,000] than £1-million [$2,801,000]. The final figure was £2,631,000 [$7,-369,431], the loss being shared by eight banks. The

National Provincial, with £1,100,000 [$3,080,000] on the train, was the biggest loser.

An official of the British Insurance Association said it was possibly the biggest single loss for the insurance market outside a major disaster such as the wreck of a great ship or two jet airliners crashing.

Only the Midland Bank could not claim insurance and had to bear its loss of £500,000 [$1,400,500]. A company spokesman defended their policy of posting notes uninsured by saying that the saving in insurance premiums over the years adequately covered the loss. As the rate for insuring banknotes averages about 1s 3d. [$.17] per £1,000 [$2,801], the saving to the Midland on this particular run would have been £31 5s. [$86.90]!

THE BANDITS'
LAIR

2

On the day after the robbery, when the banks had published their losses, the two London firms of loss adjustors handling the insurance claims offered a reward of £200,-000. This brought the total reward offered to £260,000 as the Midland Bank and the G.P.O. had made independent offers of £50,000 and £10,000 respectively.

The terms of the reward were that it would be paid to the first person giving information leading to the arrest of the thieves and the recovery of the stolen money or a proportion of it. The bait was so large that both the police and the adjustors were confident that it was only a matter of days or even hours before one of the gang squealed. But, unfortunately, no squealer came forward. In fact the police had to rely on their own routine work and the help of the public in every major aspect of the case.

The Postmaster-General made another statement on the same day revealing that the three top-security coaches which should have been on the mail run on the night of the robbery were all out of action. Some six weeks earlier one had been withdrawn with a hot axle. Ten days later a second coach went out with the same trouble. A week before the raid the third coach was found to have a "flat tire"—which meant that the metal wheel was no longer circular.

Mr. Bevins said he could not rule out the possibility that the coaches had been deliberately sabotaged, although he thought it unlikely.

"But I am shocked and disturbed at the apparent delay in getting these top-security coaches back into service," he added. "If one of these coaches had been on the hijacked train it may not have foiled the robbery but it would certainly have made the thieves' task more difficult."

16

The authorities have since satisfied themselves that the coaches were not tampered with and deliberately put out of action. The coincidence seems almost too good to be true, for experts estimate that it would have taken the robbers at least half an hour to hack their way into one of the anti-bandit coaches. That extra half-hour could have meant the difference between success and failure.

The scene of the crime yielded little. An abandoned airfield nearby was examined for evidence of a recent landing and take-off in the belief that the money may have been flown abroad. The results were negative. Plaster-casts of lorry tire marks were taken in a field near the robbery and the police toyed vaguely with the idea of reconstructing the crime.

In London plain-clothes men visited clubs, pubs and criminal haunts for evidence of free spending. They also searched for the men they suspected, without definite proof, of having committed a daring £62,500 [$175,062.50] wages robbery at London Airport the previous November. The mail robbery bore the same hallmarks of careful planning and original thinking.

In the airport raid three of a gang of nine men disguised themselves in the uniform of "city gents" with umbrellas, bowler hats and spectacles, and waited unchallenged by the elevator on which the wages would be loaded. Five of their accomplices concealed themselves in an upper floor so that they could watch the progress of the trolley pulling the banknotes to the lift. Then they summoned the lift, got inside it and, when security men accompanying the wages pressed the button for the elevator, came down in it, masked. With the help of the three "city gents" they knocked out the guard and escaped in two waiting Jaguar cars with their loot.

Only one man was convicted for the wages robbery. The police were confident that they knew who the others were and unless they could provide cast-iron alibis for their movements on August 7 and 8 they would be number one suspects.

The name of Billy Hill was, inevitably, dragged into the investigations. Hill, now the owner of a number of thriving business enterprises, was the self-confessed king of London's underworld for some years after the war. A book he wrote on his criminal exploits was a best-seller. From his yacht in Cannes where he was entertaining a number of friends the ex-gang leader stoutly denied that he was in any way involved in the train robbery.

He also threatened to take legal action against anyone implicating him and his name dropped out of the case for good.

But there were other names and theories to conjecture with. There was general agreement among the Press that the robbery had been masterminded—but by whom?

As the *Daily Express* reported on August 9, "detectives trying to pick up a whisper about the latest raid in the clubs of London's underworld last night met with silence. For someone has learned to eliminate the gangster's major giveaway—his inability to keep his mouth shut. It is almost certain that one man plotted the raid. This is probably how his raids are planned. First, he gets a tip-off about a train. Usually it comes from an 'ideas' man.

"He never actually meets the leader, only his contacts. Then a small team of 'officers' are told to hand-pick the raiders. They are given a substantial cash down payment and an assurance that if they are caught their wives and families will be looked after. Contacts have to be made and bought in Glasgow, London and at the scene of the crime. Afterwards raiders go their own ways, knowing the haul will not be touched and distributed for several weeks."

Other theories flew thick and fast. On August 11 *The People* was the first newspaper to link the London Airport raid of the previous November with the Great Train Robbery. In the opinion of the crime reporter the £62,500-wage grab was merely a "curtain-raiser" to meet the expense of the mailbag "grand slam."

Another theory being probed by Scotland Yard was that the mailbag robbery was the work of the Irish Republican Army. Scotland Yard was looking for three Irishmen thought to have been in the gang, who had disappeared from Dublin. The Irish police suspected

19

them of robbing three Dublin banks in the past two years.

The *Daily Mail* announced that a baronet was being shadowed by the police. "The check was ordered when it was found that he was associated with men suspected of having taken part in the £2½-million mail robbery," wrote Owen Summers. "A chapter in the dossier being drawn up by the police is devoted to the activities of the baronet."

The most offbeat theory was advanced by Peter Gladstone-Smith.* He announced: "Detectives investigating the Great Train Robbery yesterday know the identity of the criminal who masterminded the £2,631,784 raid. He is a miser and lives alone in one room at Brighton. His home has been searched and he is being watched. There is not enough evidence yet to arrest him. This man has a flair for the most ingenious type of crime. He works with infinite care and patience to prepare a plan which is perfect in every detail. He is known to the underworld by a nickname, travels widely, and meets other criminals in the clubs which they frequent. He has a criminal record but no convictions for more than twenty years.

"This man's frugal existence and austere surroundings have defied all efforts to prove his guilt in the past. Detectives believe it has been his ambition to amass a huge sum of money; he is now expected to retire from crime.

* *Sunday Telegraph*, August 11, 1963.

"He never takes part in an operation himself. When his plan is complete he takes it to a master criminal, well known in the Harrow Road area of London, who carries it out with confederates."

On August 12 Detective-Superintendent Gerald McArthur, the senior Scotland Yard man then on the case, made an announcement to the Press, which is generally held to have been a tactical blunder. He said that in his opinion the missing money had been hidden within thirty miles of Aylesbury. Every possible hiding-place in the area was being searched by an army of police which included handlers and their dogs. The superintendent's reasoning was correct, but its effect was to panic the gang who might otherwise have been caught with the loot intact.

On the week-end after the raid John Maris, a thirty-three-year-old herdsman living in the Oakley area, had noticed strange goings-on at a farm called Leatherslade, a mile from where he worked. Leatherslade had been on the market and unoccupied for six months and Mr. Maris first became suspicious about its new occupants when he heard that they had offered £100 more than the asking price of £5,500 [$15,405.50].

The people who had taken it over never seemed to do any work, did not use the village shops and, most curious of all, they had blacked out all the windows.

On Monday, August 12, the same day that Supt. McArthur made his statement, Maris saw a lorry parked in the yard. He nosed around. In a shed he saw another vehicle with a tarpaulin draped over the windscreen and the back. He decided that the police should be told about these vehicles.

At 9:45 a.m. he telephoned the Aylesbury police. But it was not until the next day and after another phone call to the police by Mr. Maris, that a squad-car with detectives went to investigate his report that the farmhouse was the bandits' hideout. Somehow, amid the feverish activity at police headquarters in Aylesbury, the herdsman's first message had been submerged in the mass of information pouring in.

The police arrived at Leatherslade Farm at 11 a.m. on Tuesday, August 13, and they were quickly convinced that this had indeed been the bandits' lair. Outside the pale-blue front door stood a grey Landrover. Another Landrover and a bright yellow lorry, wrapped in tarpaulin, were parked in a shed screened by an apple orchard. Green, red and khaki blankets covered the white-painted windows. Behind a hedge of unpicked runner-beans was a grave-like pit, five feet deep, with a spade still sticking in the clay amid empty mailbags. More bags were scattered inside the house, while in the cellar lay a pile of wrappings marked "National Provincial Bank."

The kitchen was well stocked with tinned food, beer, tea, sugar, eggs, fruit and bread which was not yet stale. There was no furniture or linen except for a rough kitchen table, two old chairs, upturned vegetable boxes, sleeping bags and blankets. It was quite clear that the occupants had left in a panic. There were half-finished meals on the kitchen table. Nor had there been enough time to burn the mailbags and other evidence in the pit which they had dug for the purpose.

Mountains of cigarette ends and empty cigarette boxes in the six bedrooms indicated the long sleepless nights and the anxious nocturnal discussions among the lesser members of the gang as to the disposal of the loot.

There was also evidence of their boredom, frustration and strain while they were waiting in the hide-out for the heat to cool off. In the kitchen lay shattered pieces of beer bottles which had apparently been flung against the wall in outbursts of tension.

As soon as the deserted hide-out was discovered Scotland Yard virtually took over the case. Commander George Hatherill, head of the Yard's detective force, arrived at Leatherslade with twenty of his top specialists who began taking the place apart. Fingerprint experts, cameramen and forensic scientists checked it over inch by inch while other detectives quizzed everyone living in the neighborhood.

Leatherslade had been owned by Bernard Rixon, a forty-two-year-old sub-postmaster who moved exactly a month before the robbery from Leatherslade to Dunsden, near Reading. He said that after advertising the house for sale he came across a man looking at the building from a Ford Zodiac.

"He said he wished to buy it and I told him to get in touch with my solicitor at Oxford," said Mr. Rixon. "I didn't see him again."

The deal was concluded through his lawyer after the buyer, a man of about fifty, put down a tenth of the purchase price. He left the keys with his nearest neighbor, Mrs. Lily Brooks. These had been picked up, said Mrs. Brooks, on July 29 by a tall, fair, charming man dressed in an expensive sports suit.

"He was not a country man," she told the police. "He had a distinct London accent."

When handing over the keys Mrs. Brooks remarked, in friendly country fashion, "I hope you'll be very happy."

As he got into his Anglia car the man smiled. "I expect I shall be happy." Then he added significantly, "Very."

While the police gave it out—presumably in an attempt to cover up the delay in acting on Maris's first phone call to them—that the gang had left hurriedly "about three days ago or possibly only on Sunday," it seemed fairly certain that they had actually left early on the morning of Tuesday, August 13, some 17 hours after the herdsman's first report, and only a few hours before the police arrived.

The Vicar of Oakley, the Reverend Stuart Ashby, said he heard three lorries pass his vicarage toward Bicester at 3:00 a.m. that morning.

"They were being driven very quickly," he said. "My wife and I were awakened by the noise. There is an awkward bend near us and they did not appear to slow down to take it, although they must have been using only their side lights as we saw no sign of headlights. Five minutes later two cars roared past."

The gang had counted on a long stay at the farmhouse since enough food for twenty days was found in the larder. From the way the floorboards had been recently removed, and replaced, they must have buried their loot under the house as soon as they arrived.

Police scientists divided the house into sections and searched every inch of it with microscopic care. Their careful probings paid dividends. There had been an attempt to obliterate fingerprints, but the police discovered enough to compile a large dossier to send back to Scotland Yard for comparison.

The complete story of carelessness and panic began to emerge. The gang, so closely disciplined and trained for the actual raid, had behaved like amateurs once the action was over.

They must have known that police searching the area would get to the farmhouse within a few days of the raid, even without a tip-off. Yet instead of losing themselves in London and storing the money, or else leaving immediately for abroad by private plane or yacht, at least some of them planned to sit it out near the scene of the crime in a blacked-out house which would have looked suspicious to the most casual passer-by from the neighborhood.

This was wrong planning rather than carelessness, but the way in which they behaved during this last phase of the plan—touching objects with their bare hands, failing to wear gloves every minute of the day and night —amounted to recklessness.

With the discovery of the farmhouse hide-out the police were now only eight hours behind the gang who had split up, carrying among them up to two-and-a-half tons of notes.

It seemed now as if it could be only a matter of days before the entire gang was rounded up and their huge haul recovered.

THE MANHUNT
BEGINS

3

It was more a case of scrupulous honesty than dishonesty which led, ironically enough, to the first arrest and the recovery of some of the loot.

Like nearly everyone else, Mrs. Ethel Clark, a sixty-seven-year-old policeman's widow living in Bourne-mouth, had followed the events of the train robbery with great interest. But when two men, obviously Londoners from their accents, went to her home in Tweedale Road to inquire about renting the large lock-up garage next to her house, there was no thought in her mind that they might have had anything to do with the big job.

It was only when they insisted on paying her three months' rent in advance that Mrs. Clark became suspicious. Such solicitude for the landlord's interests is rare in Bournemouth where there is no overnight car parking problem. Mrs. Clark was not to know that in London a lock-up garage is so hard to find that a hefty advance on securing one is standard practice. Her suspicions were strengthened when one of the two men pulled out a thick wad of notes to pay her.

So while her callers were actually putting their van, an Austin A35, into the garage, Mrs. Clark telephoned the Bournemouth police. Two plain-clothes detectives, Sergeant Stan Davies, a burly forty-six-year-old former rugby forward, and twenty-nine-year-old Detective-Constable Charles Case, were at the house within minutes.

When they began to question the men outside the garage, there was a short but violent struggle. Sergeant Davies brought down one man with a rugby tackle; the other rushed down the road and through the open door of a private house. Case chased after him and found him crouching on the landing at the top of the stairs. He agreed to come quietly, and the two men were driven to the police station.

A search of the van revealed bundles and bundles of notes behind the back seat. Later that day the police took possession of another car parked two miles away. In a bag in the boot were more bundles of notes. Another car abandoned in the Bournemouth area and traced to the two arrested men yielded nothing.

When all the notes which had been found were stacked together at the station, the police had no idea whether they had recovered all the missing money or only a portion of it. It looked like a fortune, which indeed it was by normal standards. But a senior bank clerk who was hastily summoned reported after several hours of counting that the notes amounted to £141,017 [$394,988.61]. This was a mere fraction of the missing money . . . less than a twenty-fifth.

The two men, identified as Roger John Cordrey, of East Molesey, Surrey, and William Gerald Boal, of Fulham, London, were questioned until 4 a.m. by Mr. Malcolm Fewtrell, head of the Buckinghamshire C.I.D., and Superintendent McArthur, both of whom had hurried to Bournemouth from Aylesbury when the arrest was reported in the afternoon. The men were formally charged and taken to Aylesbury jail.

Meanwhile the Flying Squad in London made two raids. At 3 a.m., when the men in Bournemouth were reaching the end of their questioning, the police interrogated Boal's wife in Fulham. She told Detective-Sergeant John Hensley, "If you're looking for money

I may as well show you. You're bound to find it." She produced £330 in £5 and £1 notes which, she said, had been given to her the previous week-end by her husband.

Sergeant Hensley and his men then traveled fifteen miles to East Molesey to a florist's shop, the Buttonhole. The owner, Alfred Pilgrim, and his wife Florence came downstairs in dressing-gowns. After telling them that he had reason to believe that some of the missing money was on the premises the sergeant warned, "I propose to pull the place apart until I find the money." Mrs. Pilgrim thereupon produced £860 in £5 notes.

At almost the precise moment the next day when the prosecution was opening its case against the five arrested men and women before the magistrate at Linslade, a young man and woman who were exploring Redlands Wood, a beauty spot near Dorking, Surrey, saw two holdalls and a briefcase lying just off the pathway. After fruitlessly searching the area for the owner they decided to look inside the bags for an address. There was nothing to identify the owner, but inside were thousands of banknotes. The realized immediately that they must have stumbled across some of the loot from the mail train robbery.

They kept their heads admirably. While the man guarded the money, the woman walked to the roadside and flagged down a passing motorist who agreed to call the police from the nearest telephone box. When the police arrived one of the tracker dogs soon nosed out another suitcase also filled with notes. It took six hours to count the money at Dorking police station and the total was £101,000 [$282,901].

By now the police were confident that the gang were in such a panic that they might abandon the money wherever they had gone their separate ways. They issued an appeal to the public to watch out for buried treasure. They also asked people to report any large holes they may have seen being dug in isolated spots.

"There is booty to be found in all sorts of odd places," Superintendent Fewtrell declared optimistically. Throughout that week-end thousands of people combed the countryside for miles around the scene of the robbery. The police switchboard at Aylesbury was jammed with calls which came at the rate of ten a minute, about mysterious holes, evidence of recent digging, and vehicles containing holdalls on the back seat. Many an innocent farmer was surprised in the act of transplanting a tree. Enthusiastic skindivers searched pools and streams. Courting couples in cars parked in woods were kept under observation and reported. Gravel pits throughout Buckinghamshire were searched by the police, and woods near a hospital at Coulsdon, Surrey, were combed after patients reported that they had seen men carrying suitcases in among the trees.

But in spite of confident official statements that the bandits had become embarrassed by the immensity of their haul and must be dumping or burying it in small amounts the searchers found nothing further.

There was, however, one interesting development that week-end when police discovered a black 1961 Austin Healey sports car near London Airport. The car had been bought for cash at the Chequered Flag Garage in Chiswick on August 9, the day after the robbery. Among the £5 notes handed in payment to Mr. Richard James, the garage's assistant buyer, were some whose serial numbers had been circulated by the police. The couple who bought the car were described as a tall, bespectacled, smartly-dressed man of about thirty-five and a plump, shabbily-dressed woman with a badly pitted complexion and a distinctive East London accent.

The car was discovered at Hayes, Essex, outside the home of Mrs. Phyllis Evans, owner of a garage business at nearby Harlington, nine days later. An employee of hers, Mr. Gayner Chalcroft, remembered the car being left there by a man whose description tallied in every way with that given by Mr. James. The man had explained that he was going to catch a plane at London Airport and that he would ring the garage on his return in September so that Mr. Chalcroft could drive it out to him.

"He got into a friend's car and drove off in the direction of the airport," Mr. Chalcroft told the police.

The car might have remained unnoticed at the Harlington garage for many weeks had it not been necessary, on August 17, to have the forecourt cleared because of reconstruction work. Mrs. Evans drove the Austin Healey to her home and parked it outside. It was soon spotted there by keen-eyed patroling policemen who had the registration number.

The man and the woman involved in this car episode were quickly identified from police photographs as Bruce Richard Reynolds, a forty-one-year-old antique dealer, and Mrs. Mary Kazih Manson, a forty-two-year-old housewife of Wimbledon Close. Their names and descriptions, as well as those of several others wanted for questioning in connection with the train robbery, were published in the *Police Gazette* and circulated to Britain's 75,000 policemen. But it was to be several days before the public were asked to help them in their hunt.

Reynolds' description and that of another man, James White, were issued to the Press on August 22, the day on which Mrs. Manson was arrested and charged with receiving £835 stolen from the mail train.

Throughout the evening of August 22 television programmes were continually interrupted to screen pictures and descriptions of Reynolds and White. The latter, a forty-three-year-old café proprietor with staring eyes, was probably accompanied by a woman, a baby and a poodle called Gigi, said the police.

They obviously believed that it was White who had abandoned a caravan on a site in the Dorking area eight miles from the spot where the £101,000 [$282,901] was found. The caravan bore every sign of having been left in a hurry. Other caravan owners on the site reported that it had been occupied by a man and a woman with a poodle and a baby in a carry-cot. A cursory examination on the spot revealed nothing incriminating in the caravan, but when it was stripped down at police workshops it was found to be literally papered with banknotes. In the space between the metal outside walls and the inner lining £30,000 [$84,030] had been skilfully and painstakingly inserted. This was the work of a real craftsman, said an admiring police spokesman.

At the same time the police announced that they had completed their examination of the hide-out farm where they had found the fingerprints of fifteen people. They now had a suspect list of twenty men who had not been seen in their usual haunts since the robbery, and the hunt was really on. Scotland Yard stopped all leave for Flying Squad men who were carrying out a series of raids on houses and clubs, mainly in South London.

Gigi, the white poodle believed to be accompanying White, caused the loss of thousands of man hours to police forces throughout the country. Reports that the dog had been spotted poured in and each alarm had to be investigated. But every white dog picked up by the police as a possible "suspect" was claimed by anxious— and innocent—owners.

The description of a well-known racing driver wanted in connection with the raid was circulated on August 23. Only the day before, this man, Roy John James, known as "The Weasel," had made himself hot favorite for the *News of the World* formula junior race which was to be run at Goodwood on August 24. In his 1,098 c.c. blue and white Brabham Ford which he had entered for the race, he put in the day's fastest practice lap of 95.57 m.p.h.

It seems likely that if Scotland Yard had held its hand until the day of the race its men would have picked him up there. James was known to be such an enthusiast for the sport that, after his successful practice run, he would almost certainly have gone to Goodwood to take part in the race.

In fact, even after announcing that he was wanted for questioning, the police were so hopeful he would still turn up to race or at least watch, that dozens of plain-clothes men mingled with pit crews and racing fans. Not surprisingly, James kept away.

A thirty-one-year-old bookmaker, Charles Frederick Wilson, became the seventh person in the case to be arrested. As with the other accused, the evidence against him when he appeared before the Linslade magistrate was formal. But it included a picturesque piece of underworld slang which so took people's fancy that in the months since the trial it has passed into more general usage. Superintendent Butler said that after he had been questioned at Cannon Row police station Wilson said, "You obviously know a lot. I've made a ricket somewhere. I'll have to take my chance. I don't see how you can make it stick without the poppy—and you won't find that."

A ricket, the superintendent explained, meant "mistake," while "poppy" was a word for money.

During their investigations the police had several times interviewed Brian Arthur Field, the twenty-nine-year old managing clerk for the London firm of solicitors who handled the purchase of Leatherslade Farm. On September 10 they arrested him and a thirty-one-year-old merchant seaman of the same surname, Leonard Dennis Field. The two men were not related.

From the earliest days of the investigation, the name of Douglas Gordon Goody, thirty-two-year-old owner of a women's hairdressing business in Putney, was one which cropped up in newspaper stories. Goody had stood trial for the London Airport wages robbery of 1962 but was acquitted by the jury after establishing an alibi.

In August, about two weeks after the train robbery, he was traced to a hotel in Leicester where detectives knocked him up at 2 a.m. and took him to local police headquarters for questioning. Later he was taken to Aylesbury where he was held and interrogated for thirty-six hours by Superintendent Butler. The girl he had been visiting in Leicester, nineteen-year-old Margaret Perkins, who had recently won the title of Miss Midlands, was questioned about the money in her possession, amounting to £25, and about the £2,250 [$63,-022.50] mink-covered studio couch at her home. But if the police entertained suspicions that this indicated a style of living not in keeping with Miss Perkins' provincial background, they were soon put right. She explained that both the money and the couch were trophies from the beauty contest the previous Wednesday.

Goody was released, but sixteen days later, at the request of the police, he drove to Aylesbury from London in his white sports car, one of his fleet of three vehicles which included a 3.8 Mark II Jaguar. When he left the Buckinghamshire headquarters fifteen minutes after arrival, he told waiting newspapermen: "I suppose I was interviewed because I know some of the boys the police are interested in over the train robbery. I told the police where I was on that particular night and it must have satisfied them."

A week later after a further visit to Aylesbury he was complaining to the Press that the police seemed to believe he was a "big man" in the train robbery.

"In fact," Goody declared, "I'm not even a small man. I have nothing to do with it at all. I don't mind it so much for myself, but there's my mother to think of. When she looks out of the window the chances are there's a detective outside. When I go out it's a certainty that one is following me. Anyone would think that I was one of the train robbers.

"I got pulled in when £62,000 was stolen at London Airport last year. The police really believed I was in on that job, but I was cleared at the Old Bailey."

As for arresting him it was a case of now or never. "Either they charge me today or they get off my back," he asserted.

He was arrested and charged two weeks later.

There came a strange development in the manhunt when Scotland Yard called a Press conference and newspapers were asked to publish as prominently as possible the next day pictures of one of the five wanted men, Ronald "Buster" Edwards, and his wife June. Edwards, a man of thirty-one, was well known in boxing and racing circles. His wife, an attractive brunette, had been judged beauty queen of an Isle of Wight holiday camp six weeks before the train robbery. While asking the co-operation of newspapers, the police requested the BBC and Independent Television authorities not to transmit pictures of the Edwardses or breathe a word in their news bulletins about the "trap" being laid.

The reasoning behind this move was that Edwards and his wife, if they were still in London (as the police believed), would realize that the heat was on them again if the "wanted" appeal was put out over the air. If holed up, their main source of information would obviously be radio and television. The Yard's hope was that before they got hold of a newspaper on the morning of publication someone would have remembered seeing them and would inform the police.

The radio and TV authorities complied with the request and every morning newspaper displayed pictures of the couple, but nothing came of this elaborate but somewhat ill-conceived plan. It might have been more rewarding to have asked the millions of televiewers who rarely read a newspaper to co-operate.

ROOFTOP
CHASE

4

By the middle of September the police believed they were hot on the trail of Roy "The Weasel" James. A Morris 1000 car belonging to him was found abandoned on a grass verge near Ealing, its headlights blazing. A house-to-house search in the area, however, proved fruitless.

Another arrest was made in October. Mr. John Denby

Wheater, a well-known London solicitor who was Brian Field's employer, was arrested for conspiracy and harboring Leonard Field, the merchant seaman accused in the case. He joined the accused in the dock at Aylesbury, but was allowed bail of £15,000. The case against him was concerned almost entirely with Leatherslade Farm and the negotiations leading up to its sale.

Wheater was to have been called as a Crown witness but after further inquiries, the prosecution "took a much more sinister view as to his complicity in the whole affair."

The preliminary inquiry occupied twenty-nine sittings spread over a period of nine weeks. It ended on December 2, when eighteen of the nineteen accused were sent for trial at Aylesbury Assizes.

The case against Mrs. Mary Manson was dropped, and the court agreed that she should be awarded costs out of public funds. The eleven men accused of actually taking part in the robbery were remanded in custody, while the remaining seven, who were charged with receiving and other counts, were allowed bail.

The evidence throughout the hearing had been mainly forensic and the repetition of verbal statements alleged to have been made by the accused to various investigating officers. Some £2,300,000 [$6,442,300] was still missing, as indeed were the five men named by the police as major suspects (Reynolds, Edwards, James, White

40

and John Thomas Daly, brother-in-law and partner in an antique shop of Reynolds).

The atmosphere of anti-climax which had gradually stifled interest in the case during the preliminary inquiry was broken on December 3, the day after it ended.

Shortly after 4 o'clock in the afternoon, six carloads of police swooped on a flat in one of London's most fashionable districts, Eaton Square in Belgravia. There in a £45-a-week apartment they found Daly and his wife. Superintendent Butler, for one, could hardly believe that the slim bearded man now facing him in the well-furnished room was the plump smooth-cheeked man they had hunted for four months.

Daly and his wife had been tenants there for nearly two months.

The caretaker, Mr. Bill Farrow, told reporters he knew them as Mr. and Mrs. R. J. Grant. He had never seen the husband; "Mrs. Grant" told him that her husband was in hospital after a heart attack. The caretaker was asked by her to give two short knocks if ever he wanted to see her.

Superintendent Butler, who led the squad of raiding detectives, borrowed Mr. Farrow's passkey to get inside the Dalys' one-room flat. Daly had lost thirty pounds in weight, while his wife was so heavily pregnant that she too was almost unrecognizable from her description.

At first Daly denied that he was the man they were

after. "My name is Grant," he insisted to the detectives. Inspector Williams, who had known him in the past, told him that he knew he was Daly in spite of his beard and loss of weight. Eventually Daly said, "Yes. You've got me."

When the police told him that his fingerprints had been found at Leatherslade Farm, the hideout of the train robbers, Daly interrupted them. "You're wasting your time," he protested. "I've never been to that bloody farm. I'm not being awkward. That's the truth. I expected you sooner or later, but you aren't taking my wife, are you?"

The police, showing considerable humaneness, did not even question Mrs. Daly and allowed her to leave with her brother.

Eight days after Daly's arrest there were two sensational developments on the same day. "The Weasel" was arrested in St. John's Wood, London, after a dramatic rooftop chase, and £50,000 [$140,050] was found in two sacks in a telephone booth following a tip-off to Scotland Yard by an anonymous informer. This brought the total amount of recovered money to more than £300,000 [840,300].

James had been on the police wanted list since the end of August and the hunt for him had spread over seventy-six counties. Yet neighbors said that he had lived in the mews cottage at No. 14 Ryder's Terrace, some three miles from Scotland Yard, for six months.

The house was let to a tall, dark, well-dressed man whose description fitted Bruce Reynolds. This man and James had shared the cottage and received many visitors. The neighbors were curious and noticed that all the morning newspapers and six to ten pints of milk were delivered daily.

One woman, Mrs. Deirdre Holloway, told reporters how a mysterious Chinaman called so frequently on the two men without ever getting a reply that she and her husband used to weave stories about the odd set-up at No. 14. But with true British respect for minding their own business none of the people in the neighboring cottages reported any suspicions they might have had.

The tip which sent a force of thirty policemen headed by Superintendent Butler to the mews cottage came from the underworld. They rapidly sealed off the area, then hammered on the door of No. 14. There was no reply, but the figure of a man was seen peering from behind a curtain on the first floor.

Two detectives were hoisted to a small first-floor balcony. They smashed a window and charged into the room where the man had been seen. But their quarry was just disappearing through a fanlight on the roof. He ran along the entire length of the top of the terraced cottages clutching a holdall. Reaching the end of the buildings he jumped into a back garden almost into the arms of the policemen on the ground.

Like Daly, James had grown a beard. James denied

that the holdall had anything to do with him. It contained £12,041 [$33,726.84] in notes. Two of these were £5 notes which could be traced to the robbery. They had been marked by a bank clerk in Inverness on August 6 for despatch to the head office in London of the National Commercial Bank of Scotland.

It was alleged by the police that fingerprints belonging to both James and Daly were found at the farm. Daly's appeared on the imitation money used in the game of *Monopoly* while James's appeared on a cat's dish.

It is generally believed that had the police not been in such a hurry to arrest James and had they waited a little longer they would have also found Reynolds. It was reported that he would arrive at Ryder's Terrace between 8 and 8:30 p.m. If he did, in fact, go anywhere near the neighborhood after James's arrest at 7:30 p.m. he must have heard about the Weasel's capture and reacted accordingly.

Anthony Lejeune, the scholarly crime-writer for the *Sunday Times*, wrote, "The principal planner of the great train robbery in August nearly walked into a police trap at a house in Highgate, London, last week. The police have been almost certain of the man's identity for some time. He is known to be an 'intellectual' and speaks with a soft Cockney accent. He is tall, in his thirties, and habitually wears horn-rimmed glasses. . . ."

For reasons best known to himself Mr. Lejeune

changed the setting of the incident from St. John's Wood to Highgate nearby.

Scotland Yard had believed for some time that the tall, bespectacled but tough Reynolds might be the most important man on their wanted list. The West German Police had given them a lead when a surgeon in Hamburg reported that a man whom he was able almost positively to identify from photographs as Reynolds offered £9,000 [$25,209] in sterling for quick plastic surgery to alter the shape of his mouth. The man, who spoke English, claimed to be a Dane.

The surgeon said he would have to consider, and the man left a hotel address. When the police arrived at the hotel, he had gone. Since then he has been reported to be in so many places in different countries that in spite of his height of 6 ft. 1 in. and his distinctive appearance, it seems as if he is able to move through Britain and the Continent unchallenged, always several jumps ahead of the police.

The arrest of James four months and two days after the robbery was the last real development in the case up to the time the trial opened before a judge on January 20. There were, however, a number of interesting and amusing sidelights which, even during the dullest periods of the preliminary hearing and after, kept the case constantly before the public.

The robbery had so captured American interest that the magazine *Life* made an eight-page reconstruction of the raid. Using three reporters, three photographers and a team of office boys and their friends, Mr. Tim Green, the magazine's London correspondent, staged a train hold-up.

While the police agreed to co-operate to some extent, they would not allow Mr. Green and his helpers to stop a train at Sears Crossing. So this enterprising journalist used one of the old steam engines and Victorian coaches on the Bluebell Line, that stretch of track in Essex which is privately owned and operated by a group of enthusiasts who so mourn the passing of coal-fire puffers and their regally equipped carriages that they keep the tradition alive in this way.

The American branch of Landrover launched an advertising campaign which boasted that the train robbers used their vehicles.

"We are strictly on the side of law and order," the advertisement said. "But can you blame us for feeling a certain warm glow when we read that the perpetrators of England's greatest robbery also chose a Landrover to do the job?

"The Armed Services of twenty-six countries used the Landrover, the police forces of thirty-seven, legions of country squires, desert chieftains, titled people and oil prospectors. Not to mention sportsmen and all sorts of nice families who use them for skiing.

"But what a marvellously splendid proof of the pud-

46

ding it is that the chaps who pulled off the Great Train Robbery were equally discerning."

Mrs. Ethel Clark, whose threepenny phone-call led to the recovery in Bournemouth of £141,000 [$394,941], announced that any reward money she got would go to charity.

At the same time, Mr. Bernard Rixon, owner of Leatherslade, was handed back his property and decided to go into the exhibition business. For 2s. 6d., children half-price, it was now possible to see the bandits' hide-out.

Meanwhile the villagers of Oakley, the nearest community to the farm, were infuriated by Mr. Roger Gresham-Cooke, the controversial young Tory Member of Parliament in whose constituency Oakley fell. He told a meeting of Young Tories at Westminster that in his opinion Mr. Maris, the herdsman whose tip led to the discovery of the secret of Leatherslade, and his neighbors had been negligent.

They should have been more "nosey" about the occupants of the farmhouse. He recalled that Mr. Maris had not noticed anything suspicious until four days after the robbery, when he had told the police.

"Mr. Maris must have told someone else," commented the M.P. "Why did not some farmer leave his tractor in the narrow 700-yard lane and make a further inquiry? He would have brought off the biggest criminal capture in history. But nothing was done by anyone all that Monday in the Buckinghamshire village. Weeks of effort by thousands of policemen would have been saved and the inhabitants might have had the whole reward of £250,000 themselves."

There was a Common Law duty on citizens, Mr. Gresham-Cooke declared, not only to stop crime if they could but actually to arrest criminals caught in the act.

It was one of the most extraordinary pieces of reasoning in the history of the case, and there can have been few who disagreed with Mr. Maris's opinion of his M.P. when told of the speech.

"He's just a blooming armchair hero," he scoffed. "I did what any sensible man would do. I phoned the police and kept the place under observation. The only people I mentioned my suspicions to were my employer and my wife. The boss was just going on holiday and I especially told the wife not to gossip about my discovery."

As nobody else in the village knew that anyone had moved to the farm, there was never any chance of their sharing the reward money.

But of all the crop of amusing stories which resulted from the train robbery perhaps the best was one which involved the Queen's Household Cavalry and a Mayfair nightclub hostess, Anese Adell. Miss Adell fell in love with a horse called Joe in Hyde Park when she was taking a friend's dog for a walk at dawn. Joe, who belonged to

Major Ben Wilson, a Blues squadron commander, was being exercised at the same time.

Miss Adell went straight across to the cavalry barracks opposite and told the orderly officer that she wanted to buy Joe. When she flourished a fairly thin wad of £5 notes, the officer discreetly sent a groom to telephone the police.

Detectives arrived in a police car within minutes, but after examining all the astonished hostess's fivers, they were able to assure all concerned that she was in the clear. As she said afterwards, "£55 would have been a pretty mean cut if I'd helped to steal two and a half million pounds."

Driver Mills, the man who defended his footplate with such vigor and took such a severe beating that he was still not fully recovered, was presented with £25 and a certificate recording his "courage and resource" from his grateful employers, British Railways. He was also named as one of Britain's "Men of the Year" and invited to a slap-up luncheon at the Savoy Hotel.

Regulations were waived at Aylesbury Gaol to allow Goody's Alsatian dog Sheena, who was reported to be "pining to death," to see her master. The prison governor arranged for the reunion to take place in one of the interview rooms, an appropriate comment on the spirit of Christmas, which was getting near.

Any hopes that the men awaiting trial might enjoy a home-cooked Christmas dinner were dashed a few days before Christmas Day. During a routine check of gifts for prisoners an officer found a radio battery hidden in a chicken that had been left for one of the men accused of robbing the train. It was thought that the men might be planning a mass escape over Christmas using a transistor radio set as a voice link with outside helpers.

A security clampdown was ordered and visitors were told that flasks of soup and coffee, roast potatoes, bottles of milk, puddings and other such luxuries were banned.

Mrs. Daly, who was staying with her old friend Mrs. Manson at Wimbledon, gave birth there to a nine-pound son. She announced that she would take him to see his father at Aylesbury as soon as possible and that she would not give him a name until her husband decided on one. Mrs. Manson had a fairly full house, for she also had staying with her the two children, aged two years and eighteen months, of Mrs. Bruce Reynolds, Mrs. Daly's sister.

The Post Office announced extra security precautions to guard Christmas mail. Special investigation officers, they said, would use "secret methods" to prevent thefts. They were also working on new techniques learned from America to beat any future mailbag robbers.

A survey by David Leitch of the *Sunday Times* revealed, however, that the lesson of the Great Train Robbery had still not been learned. At Manchester Exchange Station, it was claimed, any of the mailbags could have been rifled.

"I loitered for nearly twenty minutes near wagons stacked with mail and saw no-one. They were still unattended when I left to call an inspector.

"He said, 'All the trains are continually under inspection. Let's go into one of the vans together and see if we are challenged.' We did. We stood inside for five minutes. No-one came along. The inspector said, "It's because I'm here'."

Thinking that this might be an isolated mistake, Leitch asked a reporter in Glasgow to look at Central Station. The reporter found that the 6:50 p.m. mail train to London—the one robbed on August 8—was still leaving at the same time.

"It was all very casual," he wrote. "There were mountains of bags, and it would have been easy to slip into one of the open carriages and hide behind the bags."

It was the same story at Brighton and Paddington, in spite of Post Office protests that things had changed.

51

ON TRIAL

5

In the foregoing chapters we have set the scene and presented the characters for what was to be one of the longest trials in legal history.

Twenty of the accused—seventeen men and three women—originally filed into the specially constructed spike-topped mahogany dock in Aylesbury's year-old

Rural District Council offices at 10:27 a.m. on the first day, Monday, January 20, 1964.

The number was shortly reduced to twelve men, the other eight being "put down" for a later date.

Enter the judge, portly Mr. Justice Edmund Davies, through the same door as the accused.

The room buzzed with speculation. The public gallery, with seating accommodation for sixty people, was packed. The Press seats overflowed with foreign correspondents and Fleet Street's ace court reporters.

Outside television cameras still whirred. Disappointed queuers stayed put, anticipating a place inside during the afternoon.

Inside the court there was an impressive array of nearly forty counsel—among them twelve QCs—and their advisers. They occupied the center of the court room.

Preliminary troubles were soon ironed out. The microphone in the witness box received final adjustments.

At precisely 10:27 a.m., the closely guarded dock came to life as twenty pairs of eyes darted around the court room and up to the public gallery above seeking out familiar faces.

Silence. Again the focus was on the dock as the twenty accused rose to answer the charges against them.

"Guilty!" rang out twice during the thirty-minute reading of the indictment—from florist Roger John Cordrey, forty-two, to charges of conspiring to rob the Glasgow-Euston mail train and three charges of receiving stolen money.

He stood down from the dock with the seven other accused facing lesser charges, after a plea of "not guilty" had been accepted by the judge concerning Cordrey's reply to the robbery charge.

Twelve men were left in the dock and they sat in two rows of six.

All protested their innocence.

Engineer William Gerard Boal, Charles Frederick Wilson, a bookmaker, Thomas William Wisbey, bookmaker, painter James Hussey, seaman Leonard Denis Field, Douglas Gordon Goody, hairdresser, solicitor John Denby Wheater, Brian Arthur Field, managing clerk, club proprietor Robert Welch, Roy John James, silversmith, Ronald Arthur Biggs, carpenter, and antique dealer John Thomas Daly.

There was a sensational start to the trial when Mr. Ivor Richard, one of the team defending Brian Field, announced that he would challenge the entire all-male jury on the grounds that some of them might be prepared to give a corrupt verdict.

He claimed that an approach had been made to Field's lovely twenty-four-year-old German-born wife, Karen.

"In the last week," said Mr. Richard, "three approaches have been made to the wife of Brian Field by a gentleman who said a friend of his had either seen or actually had a list of possible jurors who might be called in this trial, and that five of these jurors would be prepared to give a verdict in favor of Brian Field provided they were paid."

A hushed court heard Mrs. Field tell of a visit to her village home six days previously by a man who refused to give his name, but who said he could help her husband by approaching jurors.

When she asked him in, he told her: "I know a man who has three very great friends who are going to be jurors on the case of your husband."

The mysterious caller refused to name his friend but said he was a councilor in Aylesbury. This man had access to the list of the panel of jurors. He knew five of them and three were "his very best friends." He wanted money for this service but was not prepared to name a figure.

She agreed to meet the man again on the following Tuesday at 8:00 p.m. outside Reading Station.

Before leaving her, said Mrs. Field, her visitor warned her "If this conversation goes beyond the four walls of this room you are endangering yourself and me."

The following day, however, after seeing her solicitor, she reported the visit and conversation to Det. Chief Superintendent Butler. He advised her to keep the appointment at Reading and to show interest in the proposition.

At the subsequent meeting the man told her he wanted

£8,000 [$22,408], £1,500 [$4,201.50] of which was to bribe the jurors.

"I told him that it would be necessary for me to know the name of at least one of the jurymen as a guarantee," Mrs. Field continued. "I was ordered to say that by Mr. Butler. The man said he could give me a name right now but first he wanted to consult the other man—his friend —and would let me know at the next meeting."

When he went into the witness box Superintendent Butler allayed any fears that anyone on the jury had been got at. After witnessing the meeting between Mrs. Field and a man at Reading Station, he interrogated the man at length.

"He was wanting to act as an agent provocateur, as I see it," said the police officer. "I think that, as he knows very slightly one of the accused, he was trying to get himself into a group of criminals and crime that otherwise he would know nothing about. At the back of his mind was the thought of some reward in one form or another in the event of a favorable verdict on Brian Field."

He made every effort to establish a link between the man and a certain councilor at Aylesbury but could not establish any contact between the two men.

Mrs. Field's visitor remained anonymous to the court but the superintendent wrote his name down on a piece of paper for the judge.

Finally, Mr. Justice Davies announced that he did not think reasonable grounds had been made out for suspecting the integrity of the jury. When the jury had been sworn in, however, he warned them to be on their guard.

"Sometimes," he added, "evil persons who have unworthy motives are out to wreck a trial and deliberately engage a juror in conversation about the case he or she is trying and then promptly take steps to have the juror accused of improper conduct."

The possible consequences of that might be that the whole jury would have to be discharged.

"You can realize the enormous amount of extra time and expense that will involve for everyone. I have not the slightest reason for thinking that any such interference, either innocent or malevolent, will be attempted in the course of the present trial, but unfortunately such incidents are by no means unknown in the long history of our law."

It took Mr. Arthur James, QC, leading the Crown's team of four more than ten hours to outline the case.

He recalled vividly the incident of the early hours of Thursday, August 8, 1963, and one by one proceeded to deal with each of the accused's alleged part in the plot.

On the second day, outlining the case against hairdresser Douglas Gordon Goody, the prosecutor injected the first touch of humor into the case—when he referred to the husky six footer as "Goody Two Shoes" because of paint found on a pair of his brown suede shoes. It was said to be the same color and composition as that found on get-away vehicles used by the bandits and discovered at Leatherslade Farm—yellow paint and khaki paint.

Day number three introduced the first of the prosecution's procession of two hundred and six witnesses who would appear over the next thirteen days.

A sense of expectancy filled the paneled well-lit court chamber as the usher called: "Mr. Jack Mills."

A lean man, graying and looking older than his fifty-seven years, entered the court. It was Jack Mills, driver of the ambushed train.

Unsteady on his feet, and sometimes inaudible in his speech, the witness gripped the top of the stand and only seconds later left the box.

He was allowed to sit in a chair while he gave his evidence and the microphone was lowered to him—the man who after twenty-two years as an engine driver would never be at the controls again.

Looking pale and strained, Mr. Mills wiped his brow, sipped at a glass of water as he recalled the events of that night.

He was unable to identify any of the raiders as he glanced at the thirteen men sitting in the dock.

Mr. Justice Edmund Davies, a mild-mannered personality, broke the calm of the improvised assize court on the sixth day with a reprimand.

Detective-Sergeant John Swain of Scotland Yard gave evidence, and a little later left the paneled witness stand shame-faced.

The sergeant recalled a search he made at the home of one of the accused men, Douglas Gordon Goody of Commondale, Putney, without a search warrant.

Goody's mother was the only person at home that day in the middle of August, 1963, and Goody's diminutive defender, Mr. Sebag Shaw, QC, seethed with anger at the detective's deception.

He asked Detective-Sergeant Swain: "Were you told to search the house without a search warrant?"

The detective replied: "If Mrs. Goody had said, 'You can't come in,' we would have got a search warrant."

But he admitted he had told Mrs. Goody he possessed one.

"It was a mistake, not a lie," countered Detective-Sergeant Swain. "I had other warrants to search other houses on me and I was told to go to Goody's home."

The judge snapped, "See it never happens again."

"There was no reason for searching the house at this stage. That was why there was no warrant," contended Goody's counsel.

The mystery of the missing witness was the next development in the trial.

There was no response to the usher's call "Mr. Jack Knowles." He was to have been the Crown's 124th witness.

White-haired Mr. Niall McDermott, QC, second-in-command of the prosecution's team, gave the news:

"Since he was warned to appear here he has disappeared from his home."

An out-of-court police dash to London ended with a bemused, petite lady entering the court—Jack Knowles' mother, Mrs. Margaret Knowles.

"I don't know where my son is," she told the judge.

"He knew he had to attend court," she added.

Knowles, twenty-three, a painter, was the man who had gone on a holiday trip to Ireland with Goody and his mother a few days before the train hold-up.

The judge refused to issue a bench warrant. He simply hoped that Mr. Knowles would "be more mindful of his obligations." Nothing more was heard of the missing witness. Jack Knowles' whereabouts remained a mystery.

The next piece of news was that the judge had received an anonymous letter.

Stern-faced he revealed to surprised counsel, Press and jury, at the start of the ninth day: "When this case started I thought it desirable to say a word to the jury as to the danger of anyone trying to establish contact with them.

"That I was not being too melodramatic in that warning is illustrated by the fact that this morning I received an anonymous letter which claims to instruct me in the manner in which I should carry out my duties in this trial.

"Such a person is doing a grossly improper thing.

"If such a thing was sent to the jury then that person would be guilty of a grave criminal offense.

"I say this to warn anyone who writes any letters of this kind that they will be followed up."

Gradually, vital links connecting the eleven neatly dressed men in the dock started coming to light—a little knob found in the possession of William Boal. A little knob which contained in the grooves traces of yellow paint which, according to Dr. Ian Holden, chief Scientific Officer at Scotland Yard, closely corresponded with the type of paint found at the bandits' hideaway—Leatherslade Farm.

Goody's "two shoes" were also subjected to the most intricate of scientific tests. Samples of yellow and khaki paints were comparable to that on vehicles at the farm and to a squashed tin of yellow paint on the garage floor of the lonely countryside farmhouse.

The expert's final analysis: "In theory it is possible for them to have come from different sources, but in practice highly improbable."

Day 14—Wednesday, February 6—ended on a small wave of excitement when one of the accused, Ronald Arthur Biggs, thirty-four-year-old carpenter, of Alpine Road, Redhill, Surrey, was ordered to be tried separately.

The jury was escorted from behind its rope-cordoned row of tables to the jury room at the back of the court, and a difficult legal position had a ten-minute sifting in their absence.

When the twelve silent men were back in their seats, the judge announced quietly and deliberately:

"Gentlemen, an irregularity of the most unfortunate and disastrous kind has occurred in this trial which affects one of the accused.

"And the result is that I am not going to let the trial of the accused proceed before you.

"It would not be right or just. You will be relieved of considering the case against Mr. Biggs."

Biggs was subsequently removed from his place. He had been arrested and charged with being a robber and conspirator five months earlier.

An application for bail in the judge's chambers was rejected, and Biggs was returned to the town's gray-walled prison, not more than a mile and a half from where he had sat for fourteen days.

His long wait for a separate trial started from that day.

Detective-Superintendent Maurice Ray, fingerprint expert at Scotland Yard, entered the case on Day 15.

He had gone to Leatherslade Farm shortly after it was invaded by the police on August 13. He revealed: "Large areas, particularly downstairs—the doors, win-downs, cupboards—showed signs of being wiped down."

Then men on the run had made a mess of the job, reported the eagle-eyed Yard man. Fingerprints and palm prints were in abundance.

There were many inquiring glances towards the men on trial as the expert listed the clues he had found. . . .

"Big Jim" Hussey's palm print on the tail board of a lorry in the yard . . . fingerprints of Thomas Wisbey on a bathroom rail . . . *Monopoly* tokens and the box for the game bearing John Thomas Daly's prints . . . the palm print of Robert Welch shown on a half-empty can of beer . . . Charles Wilson's palm prints on a window sill, his thumb print on a transparent wrapping, another thumb print on a drum of salt . . . Roy "The Weasel" James's hand mark on a cat's dish. And Brian Field's impression on bags containing money found in the woods at Dorking by a couple on their way to work.

The jury went on a special mission, to examine in the courtyard of the town's century old jail a Landrover— a khaki-topped and blue vehicle, 296 **POO**. This had paint on the pedals, paint similar to the markings on Goody's shoes.

On a chilly day Goody lined up with the nine other accused and watched the jurors make an inch by inch survey of the Landrover.

One by one the picture of the ten men on trial was painted by shrewd Detective Chief Superintendent Thomas Butler of Scotland Yard—the man who was behind hundreds of conferences and interviews leading to the arrest of the suspects in the case.

The past record of the smallest man on trial—Roy James—came into the open.

Mr. Butler agreed that James was a bad little fellow. "Has he got a bad character from the police point of view?" asked his counsel, Mr. William James.

"Yes," Mr. Butler replied.

The theft of a car, receipt of stolen goods (car tools and accessories), driving away a car without permission, shop-breaking and larceny—these were the offenses James had committed.

He sat passively in the dock dwarfed by prison officers and the other accused around him.

This man called "The Weasel" had been released from prison in July 1960, after a three years' spell of corrective training for the shop-breaking and larceny crime.

Goody's past was also brought up . . . his alleged involvement in the London Airport bullion raid, watch-smuggling, shop-breaking, larceny, robbery and violence, loitering with intent.

So the curtain closed on the Crown's case on Day 17, Tuesday, February 11, 1964.

Prosecution witnesses totaled a monumental 206. Exhibits were near the 600 mark. There had been almost 85 hours' talking time.

The jury was dismissed for two days. When they returned after counsel had made their submissions on Friday the 14th, one of the accused—the last to be arrested—was freed after seventy-nine days in custody. The ordeal of John Thomas Daly was over.

64

THE TRIAL
CONTINUES

6

The court was a sea of expectant faces as the judge sat back, watching the jury file into their seats at 10:57 a.m. on that day. When they were settled, he explained to the twelve 'just men' the reason for their absence of a couple of days while he listened to speeches from counsel.

"In relation to the eighth accused (John Thomas Daly), his learned counsel (Mr. Walter Raeburn, Q.C.)

has submitted to me that I ought to stop the case and I have come to the conclusion that is the right course to adopt," Mr. Justice Edmund Davies announced simply.

All eyes turned to look at the well-built and good-looking man with fair wavy hair in the dock. Daly drooped his head as though in a daze, and then stood up.

The judge added: "It would not be right for the case against Daly to proceed any further. Suspicion alone is quite insufficient."

Then the words "You are discharged" echoed round the silent court chamber, and Daly left the 'wooden prison' under a one-man guard, more than two months after being arrested. He breathed a sigh of relief outside in the courtyard. "I was innocent from the start," he announced. The ordeal had accounted for a loss in weight, to which his days in hiding also contributed. It was a man lighter by two stone who emerged into a free world.

There were now ten men left in the box, waiting to hear the legal brains fight for their innocence.

The long saga unrolled slowly. Counsel for the accused pounded relentlessly at the one vital point which was mere speculation in the Crown's case. Not one of the alleged robbers had been identified by a single witness. Not one had had the finger of recognition pointed at him. No one had said, "I saw him on the railway track on August 8."

Chubby-faced William Boal was a clever opponent in

the witness box. Parrying the bombardment of questions from the Arthur James, Q.C./Niall McDermott team, he painted a villainous picture of a man waiting to be sentenced—Roger John Cordrey, the man with whom he went to Bournemouth. Boal said he had spent money "like water," had bought a couple of vehicles with him, and arranged for accommodation in Oxford and Bournemouth.

Cordrey, an acquaintance of many years before, had, it seemed suddenly, and from out of the blue, renewed the friendship. Boal said Cordrey owed him money and that sticking to him was the only sure way of getting it back.

Boal pleaded innocent all the time. He didn't know Cheddington or Leatherslade Farm. Once he announced doggedly: "I have never been anywhere near the train spot. And if you were to offer me my freedom now, I wouldn't be able to find my way there."

Boal claimed he was the dupe of Cordrey, and that he knew nothing about the stolen money, amounting to more than £140,000, which was found in their possession when police caught them in Bournemouth.

Burly Thomas Wisbey was another of the alleged robbers and conspirators. He had to shake down evidence of a palm print on a bath rail at the bandits' countryside retreat; his own palm print. True, he had been at a farm. He admitted that. But a robber? A conspirator? Never, he said.

Where was he on the morning of the train robbery?

"In bed at my mother's house."

He was friendly with two of the other accused sitting alongside him, Robert Welch and Big Jim Hussey. He told an intriguing story of a trip into the country which he made with Welch on Saturday, August 10. It was to a lonely, isolated farmhouse to deliver vegetables with another friend of Hussey's. But was it Leatherslade Farm? Wisbey denied categorically that he knew the place he was driven to was that particular farm. It was not until much later, when under police questioning, that he realized it could have been the place.

Welch and he were taken there by a man in a lorry. All helped to unload vegetables on that afternoon. Wisbey had to wash his hands, so leaving the palm print. He shrugged off a suggestion that it was his job to wash down prints in the hide-out. "It was an innocent trip," he insisted.

Prosecution counsel brought to light an advertisement which appeared in the Personal columns of the *Evening Standard* only a couple of days earlier. It read: "Great Train Robbery. Urgent. Would anyone answering to the name of Dark Ronnie, friend of James Hussey, telephone Ellis Lincoln, Solicitor, immediately."

Two telephone numbers were given, but Wisbey said he knew nothing of the origin of the advertisement.

Dark Ronnie (his name was later to emerge as Ronald

Dark) was the key link in the stories of Wisbey, Hussey and Welch. He was the lorry driver on August 10.

Wisbey stated: "I only knew him as Ronnie, not Dark Ronnie."

Handsome Robert Welch, a man with piercing eyes —'the man of steel' was the name attributed to him by the Press—did not contest palm prints said to be his which were found on a beer can at the hide-out. He gave a more elaborate version of the ride—'an innocent one' —into the heart of Oxfordshire two days after the robbery. After a café meeting with Wisbey at the Elephant and Castle, he said, he and Wisbey went over to Hussey's house. The three of them were chatting when a lorry drove up.

"It was driven by a fellow called Ronnie," Welch said.

He was a friend of Jim Hussey's. He had to make a trip to deliver some foodstuffs. He asked Hussey to go but Hussey couldn't manage it, so instead Welch and Wisbey took the ride, following the lorry.

At the farm there were some beer cans and in Welch's own words: "They interested me. I used to be in the licensing trade and I had never seen one of these cans before. I just tilted it back to read the instructions."

This was the reason for his palm print.

Finally Jim Hussey strode to the witness stand. He knew Ronnie only by that name, he said. 'Dark' had never been used by him (Hussey) as a surname. At first

69

he said he didn't know his address. As the interrogation about Ronnie went on, the more nerves became on edge, and the negative developments seemed to irritate the judge. The apparent 'foxing' of the man in the box wasn't leading anywhere useful.

The judge stormed, "Write down the address of Ronnie."

Big Jim replied, "I don't know it."

Mr. Justice Edmund Davies: "Write down the name of the road with as many details as will enable a police officer to make inquiries this evening."

The judge fired a series of rapid questions at Hussey.

"Have you ever been inside the house?"

"Yes."

"Will you write down on this piece of paper the names of any person who can vouch for the existence of Ronnie?"

"I will, Your Lordship."

The interrogation continued into the next day. The judge persisted with the Dark Ronnie chapter, and Hussey was instructed to tell how he met him, and to broaden his statement about what happened at the Saturday meeting. This meeting had come about following a visit to Ronnie's home on Wednesday, August 7, the eve of the robbery.

Ronnie's address had now been established as being in Brixton.

Hussey said, "I caught a bus to Brixton and went to his flat. His sister and brother-in-law were there and we watched television and had some drinks. It was Ronnie's birthday. I would have arrived at about 8:45 p.m. and left at 1:30 a.m. on August 8."

They arranged to meet on the Saturday when Ronnie turned up to say he had a journey to make. Hussey was unable to go with him as his elderly mother was alone so Welch and Wisbey went instead.

It was while Ronnie's lorry was outside the house that Hussey's palm print got on the tailboard of the lorry. Hussey went to the rear and took an apple, he said.

One of the severest question-and-answer interludes to develop during the trial came when a short dark-skinned and immaculately dressed Londoner hustled to the witness box. It was Ronald Dark.

The judge stated quietly: "It is my duty to tell you that you are not obliged to answer any questions either from Mr. Brown or the prosecution or myself if you think the answers have a tendency to incriminate you."

Dark nodded responsively. He confirmed that his birthday was on August 7, 1963. He confirmed that he spent it at home at 19 Outwood House, Upper Tulse Hill, London, S.W.2. James Hussey, he agreed, spent part of the day with him, arriving at 8.30 p.m. or thereabouts, and his story tied in with Hussey's description.

They had arranged to meet on the following Satur-

71

day, but on Friday, Dark said, he met someone who asked him to do a job. "I had to deliver some goods in a lorry somewhere in Oxfordshire."

Who was the person who had asked him to do the job? It was someone called Stanley Webb, according to Dark. He had met him three or four times before, and he was to get £10 for the mission. Dark now became the subject of some harsh cross-examination by Mr. Arthur James, Q.C., a fiery interrogator. Dark agreed he had phoned Mr. Ellis Lincoln following the advertisement. Then why hadn't he come forward earlier?

"I was frightened out of my life," Dark replied.

He had no knowledge that the venue to which he went had anything to do with the train job.

And the man Stanley Webb? Dark assured everyone that he had tried to trace him, without success. But he would be only too willing to give evidence against him if he was caught.

The Ronnie Dark incident petered out. What he had said appeared to be the truth, not a concocted tale, as the Crown suggested.

Huddled in the second row of the dock, and dwarfed by his neighbors, was the silent Roy John James known as "the Weasel." He did not speak a word in his own defense, and offered no explanation for the appearance of his prints on articles at Leatherslade Farm—on a cat dish, a first-aid kit and a tin of salt. He sat always with eyes staring straight ahead.

He had had £12,041 on him when captured after a rooftop chase. But claimed his counsel, Mr. William Howard, "Over half that money, it has been proved beyond doubt, couldn't have come from the train. It wasn't issued from the Bank of England until after the train robbery."

Police witnesses revealed in court that James denied any knowledge of the hold-all containing £12,041 [$33,726.84] which fell with him when he was arrested at St. John's Wood after a rooftop chase.

"That has nothing to do with me," he had said in an aggrieved voice. And asked where he was on the night of August 7–8, his only explanation was, "Not at that farm I've read so much about."

The prosecution said that the money in James's possession on the night of his arrest, combined with figures on a scrap of paper found on him, showed that his cut of the robbery was more than £109,000 [$305,309].

"In respect of the £12,041 [$33,726.84] you will hear that many of these notes are brand new, in mint condition," said Mr. James, Q.C. "The Crown does not suggest that £12,041 [$33,726.84] is made up of notes which were actually on the train."

The Weasel had obviously changed notes from the robbery for 'clean' ones.

Mr. James said the piece of paper in the hold-all contained figures of varying amounts totaling £91,500 [$256,291.50]. Underneath these appeared the figures and letters FRA 1,000 Flat 2,000 Car 1,000—bringing the total to £95,500 [$276,495.50].

"The paper also shows the figure of £12,500 [$35,-012.50] against the name Dennis which, added to the £95,500 [$276,495.50], makes £108,000 [$302,508]," said Mr. James. "There is one further figure of £1,500 [$4,-201.50] alongside the word 'Brab' which the jury might think refers to a Brabham Ford car."

This made a grand total of £109,500 [$306,709.50].

"I say quite frankly the Crown suggests that that was James's cut of the robbery after it was shared out."

Mr. James reminded the jury that £109,000 [$305,309] had been found in three suitcases in woods near Dorking.

"You may well think that sort of money represents one man's cut of the raid."

It was the first time in the four months of proceedings in the lower court and the High Court that the prosecution had mentioned how the loot may have been shared out.

Precision driving for the getaway on the morning of the robbery was essential along the winding, narrow country lanes, and the Crown suggested James would have fitted that role well. This was rebutted by James's counsel.

James's innocence hinged on an alibi given by a stocky taxi driver, Derek Robert Brown, a fan of the Weasel's.

Mr. Brown said he was sipping coffee until 4 a.m. on

the morning of the train hold-up with James at the latter's home. He had earlier picked him up from a Chelsea night club.

The defense of burly Douglas Gordon Goody got under way on Day 25. His sprightly counsel, Mr. Sebag Shaw, opened up: "The Crown has referred to him as 'Goody Two Shoes' but I was not conscious of the fairy tale referred to." He added that he preferred to look on Goody's case as "The Paint Case." Paint found earlier on a pair of his shoes was the same as that used to paint vehicles at the farm, said the prosecution. Yellow paint. Khaki paint.

The Goody team at once implied that the paint had been planted by the police. It was a tricky point in the trial, and the judge called it "an ugly feature."

Evidence by experts on Goody's behalf claimed that the khaki paint was different, although the yellow paint could have been the same.

Where was he on the all-important night—August 7?

"In bed with my fiancée." This was petite and pretty Miss Pat Cooper, whom he was to have married at Christmas.

Goody was no angel. Even his counsel admitted that. But an angry Mr. Sebag Shaw shouted: "The maxim of giving a dog a bad name has never been better illustrated than in this case."

At the second time of asking, Goody was freed from any complicity in the mammoth London Airport bullion

75

raid which had occurred two years before. Suave, level-headed and a meticulous dresser, Goody stole the show when he entered the witness stand. His holiday trip to Ireland early in August with his mother, a widow, and the missing witness, Jack Knowles, came under examination. He had returned to London earlier than planned, on August 6 to be precise, leaving his two companions behind. Could it be that the Crown's theory that the robbery was originally arranged for August 7 was correct? And did Goody's homecoming blow his alibi sky high?

Goody remained cool. He revealed that he was in with a gang of watch smugglers; that his trip to Ireland had been for that purpose. He said he returned with 500 watches.

"Why the early return?" asked the Crown.

"I didn't want to keep the watches at my uncle's house," Goody replied.

"You didn't mention to your uncle that you cut your visit short?"

"I didn't want to mention I was smuggling watches either!" Goody riposted smartly.

He had left his mother and Jack Knowles behind because he did not want them involved if there was any trouble at the customs.

His connections with others of the accused came to light. He admitted he knew a few: Wheater and Brian

Field, because they had appeared for him during the London Airport raid trial.

He spoke of his days in hiding, and blamed the Press. They hounded him, he alleged; and he had thought the police would soon be on his tail.

"Why did you think the police would be on to you?" asked Mr. Niall McDermott.

Goody replied, "It's pretty obvious. Because every time a robbery is committed locally they pay me a visit. The police know I've got a record."

Close questioning about his association with Jack Knowles led to a surprise announcement from Mr. Arthur James, Q.C.: "It is not suggested that either Goody or Mrs. Goody is responsible directly or indirectly for the failure of Mr. Knowles to appear at this trial to give evidence. It is right to say he had given evidence at the earlier proceedings and if he had given evidence in this trial it would not have added to the case against Goody."

Brian Arthur Field spent more than a day giving his side of the story. Often he needed no prompting to launch into an explanation; he was ever willing to talk.

He admitted ownership of two of the four bags containing £100,900 [$305,309] found in the woods at Dorking. He did not dispute fingerprints said to be his on one of the bags, but said that the bags had vanished from his possession some time before the robbery. He admitted going to Leatherslade Farm with Leonard Field, the prospective purchaser. He called his boss John Wheater a hard worker "but chaotic."

According to the Crown these three figured in a conspiracy to conceal the identity of the purchaser and to obstruct the course of public justice—amending the charge from that of perverting the course of public justice.

But trouble was in store for the over-talkative Brian Field, when he was reminded of the time he was confronted with Leonard Field—at New Scotland Yard—after the robbery. Brian Field did not identify him outright as the man with whom he went to Leatherslade Farm. "He is decidedly like the man, but it's not him," Field said at the time.

He confessed that he had lied. He had been in custody for forty-eight hours when brought face to face with Leonard Field, and was all mixed up. He was concerned only with saving his own skin. He didn't want to assist the police, he told the judge and jury.

There was no kind of plot among the three of them, he claimed, occasionally glancing up towards the public gallery and smiling at his beautiful German-born wife, Karen.

She and Brian Field's ex-wife, Brenda Field, both gave evidence. The women were on good terms and they defended Field as best they could.

There next came the entrance of Leonard Denis Field, the seaman with the boyish face. The only previous conviction against him was one of being suspected of loitering, but that was when he was eighteen.

He appeared uneasy, unable to grasp the importance of the whole drama. Once he got a word of advice from the judge to assist his counsel as much as possible for his own good.

He agreed that he had been to Leatherslade Farm to look over the property. He "wasn't impressed." He had been acting in his brother Harry's interests. Harry was now behind bars.

Leonard Field's interpretation was difficult to grasp for his account was very scrappy.

But on Day 31, Monday, March 2, Leonard Field burst everything wide open. He made a sudden and dramatic confession. He discarded his "little boy lost" approach.

"I lied," he said. In between sips of water, and gripping the top of the witness box, he made a clean breast of things: "My Lord, I never learned what Leatherslade Farm was used for on August 14. I learned on August 9."

Brian Field was the man who told him, he said. Mr. Justice Davies urged Field to include every detail.

Brian Field had told him, he said, that the farm had been bought in his name (Leonard Field's) and "that I would get a substantial sum of money." In fact he was to get £5,000 if he kept his mouth shut about the Leatherslade Farm deal. But he did not get anything, he said.

"I knew I wasn't doing this for nothing, and that something would be involved. I asked him (Brian Field) there and then what would happen if anything came about with the police. I was assured I couldn't be implicated. I was told to stay away from the office and that Mrs. Wheater would take care of everything."

A meeting, which he had described earlier and which included the presence of Wheater at the scene, was sheer make-believe, he admitted. Wheater was at no meeting. There *was* no meeting. He had insisted to the police that he had never been to Leatherslade Farm at all because he thought he would be in the clear. He added that the man said to have been the purchaser of Leatherslade Farm gave no one permission to use his name.

Brian Field, called back to the box, contested every word of Field's new story.

An M.P., Mr. Paul Bryan, vice-chairman of the Conservative Party, and Brig. Geoffrey Barratt, director of Army Legal Services at the War Office, stepped into the picture. Both were called as witnesses to the character of John Denby Wheater, who had reached the rank of major during the war, but now, tired looking and older, was seated with nine other alleged criminals.

Wheater had been under the command of Mr. Bryan

on the Adriatic coast of Italy. "He was certainly brave, certainly loyal, and liked by the men," said Mr. Bryan. "His honor and integrity could not be questioned," he added.

Similar tributes were paid by the Brigadier. "A real fighting soldier," was how he summed up Wheater.

When the time came for Wheater to go into action again, this time to fight for his innocence, he was quite composed. When asked, "Do you feel that you are a person who is by nature particularly cut out to be a solicitor or not?" he answered: "I had decided some time ago that I was not, and I feel that a lot of our clients have suffered through my carelessness." He was questioned about the Leatherslade Farm deal. Wheater said the first he knew of it was when Brian Field (his managing clerk) brought Leonard Field into his office.

"Brian Field said Leonard Field wished to purchase the property and asked if I would deal with it. Leonard Field produced the particulars of sale. He merely said he was interested in buying the property and that he wanted to try to get it for less than the advertised price. He said he wanted it as quickly as possible."

Wheater went through a process of negotiations and agreed upon a price of £5,500 [$15,405.50]. "I assumed Leonard Field had seen the property, but I had no idea he had gone with Brian Field," he stated.

The basis of the trio's arguments was that Leonard Field said he was the innocent victim of two lawyers,

81

while Brian Field and John Wheater claimed they acted merely as unwitting agents of their fraudulent client Leonard Field.

The exhausting, long-drawn-out stories of the men on trial were over after seventeen days. Only one other of the accused besides James failed to utter a word in his own defense, rugged Charles Wilson. But as was frequently made clear by the judge, none of the defendants was obliged to come forward to give an explanation.

Mr. Justice Davies finally suggested a speed-up of the whole affair so that it would be over before Easter. It was at the start of the eighth week when he asked the jury if they would do some overtime by sitting on Saturdays. They readily obliged.

The final speeches were routine. Lively Mr. William Howard was one exception. He was Roy James's spokesman, and he said to the jury, "If when you go home tonight and your wife says, 'I've shot the milkman,' and you say, 'That's a good job, he has been watering the milk for months. Where's the body? Let's bury it,' you would not be guilty of murder and you wouldn't be guilty of conspiring together. You will please remember that, because it is absolutely relevant to the evidence of James."

Another imaginative talker was diminutive Mr. Joseph Grieves, the Q.C. for Thomas Wisbey. He commented on the trial in general, and compared treatment

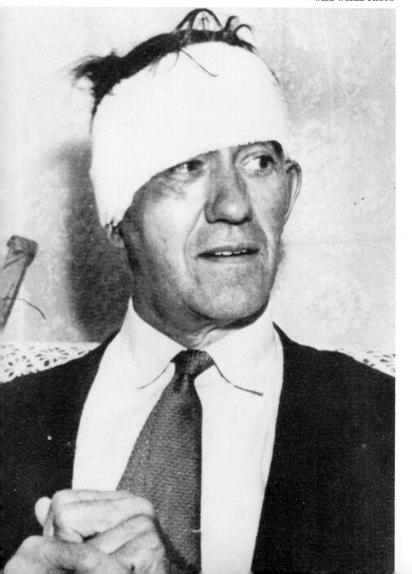

Jack Mills, the engineer of the burglarized train, talking to reporters after being released from the hospital where he was treated for wounds inflicted when he attempted to fight off the criminals.

—WIDE WORLD PHOTO

An airview of Leath-erslade Farm and the road leading away from it. The farm was eighteen miles southeast of the site of the crime.

Two sections of the looted Royal Mail train. —WIDE WORLD PHOTO

A closer view of the farm as the area is being investigated by police. Also in view—a truck the criminals left behind in their haste to flee.

—WIDE WORLD PHOTO

A sample of the "poppy," being unloaded at police headquarters at Aylesbury, Buckinghamshire.

—WIDE WORLD PHOTO

£50,000 in small notes being examined by police officers after it was found in a London phone booth following an anonymous telephone tip the night of December 10.

—WIDE WORLD PHOTO

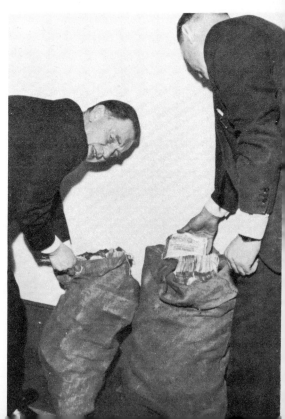

The frigate H.M.S. Russell, *which sped from Glasgow with instructions to intercept a "stolen yacht" thought to be carrying the escaped convict Charles Wilson.* —WIDE WORLD PHOTO

The aptly named Wild Venture, *the object of the* Russell's *sea search.*

—WIDE WORLD PHOTO

An amused workman replaces a wooden door through which the small gang broke to free Wilson from jail. —WIDE WORLD PHOTO

The front gate of Winson Green Prison in Birmingham. Wilson entered here, left via a different route. —WIDE WORLD PHOTO

LOOK!
OLD
BANKNOTES
ACCEPTED!

CHOICE
Canadian
Pears
2/5
2'4

BIRDS EYE
AICE FILLE

C&B
Beans
7D

In Brill, near the scene of the crime, a storekeeper with a sense of humor displays a new sign after the police had recovered some of the stolen money.

—WIDE WORLD PHOTO

of prisoners in the present day with that in the 17th century. His opinions were forthright, and effective.

"The length of this trial is something unique in my experience," he said. "I accept that this has been a most proper trial. It has been characterized by courtesy. Every accused has been addressed as mister, and yet here we are in the middle of the 20th century and you see these prisoners sitting in the dock behind spikes, just as they would have done in the 17th century. They are surrounded by prison officers. I am not saying that is not wise or necessary but four times every day—over 160 times by now—they have been taken to and from prison in a black Maria, loaded like cattle in a cattle transport, escorted by a flotilla including a busload of police officers. I am not criticizing this but I hope, with England being a civilized country, that I shall never see this again in my life. Although this may be very necessary, the more you think it is necessary the more it arouses a frame of mind against which I want you to be guarded. It is so easy to fall into the Nuremberg mentality. It is something you feel rather than consciously think. Isn't it a frame of mind in which you could say: 'Of course they are guilty. They wouldn't take all those precautions unless they were guilty?' And this trial is just a formality. I venture to put that point of view because it is possible to get ideas suggested to you subconsciously."

Shocks were still in the offing. Day 41—Monday, March 16—brought the sensation of the trial so far. One of the jurors had been offered a bribe to sway his colleagues. The hearing was abruptly halted when this was revealed. The juror involved was Mr. Terence Addy a quiet, bespectacled man, of Chalfont St. Giles.

The Chief of the Crown's team of four, Mr. Arthur James, Q.C., told the judge, "Yesterday a communication from one of the jurymen in this trial was made to the police, as a result of which he was asked to communicate with Your Lordship."

"I have the note," said the judge.

Mr. Addy rose from his chair looking nervous. The judge peered down at him. "You have been good enough to supply the court with a note relating to an incident which occurred yesterday when a stranger called upon you and made a suggestion to you, that you should for a monetary reward attempt to sway the jury in this case; and you forthwith reported the matter to the police. You have acted with absolute rectitude in the matter. It is so important that a jury should be permitted to arrive at its conclusion honestly and fairly, and the administration of the criminal law in this country is vitally dependent on this. So I am going to adjourn this case for a short time."

There was complete silence in the court.

The judge added, "I want you, in the presence of the Clerk of the Court and Mr. Fewtrell (Chief of Bucks. C.I.D.) and a shorthand writer, to go out and tell Mr. Fewtrell in the presence of these people everything you know about this incident, not for the purpose of this being made public, but so that this criminal or criminals who are attempting the ancient and still vigorous offense of embracery* may be brought to justice."

Mr. Addy was escorted to a secret room, and the jury retired to their quarters at the back of the court.

The adjournment lasted twenty minutes and when the jury took their places once more, the judge said: "I want you to dismiss absolutely from your mind this outrageous affront to your personal integrity." He then addressed Mr. Addy: "An approach of this kind is a gross insult. Before this trial began I made some remarks to you in the course of which I took the unusual course of warning you of the risk that approaches might be made by evil-minded people.

"It may have been thought in some quarters I was being melodramatic. But the incident which Mr. Addy has reported, and on which he has acted with such rectitude, illustrates I was not being melodramatic and that a warning was required. We are going to get a verdict in this case. You will, gentlemen, be more than usually punctilious during the next week so that nobody can possibly say there is anything wrong. We are going to arrive at finality in this trial."

A copy of the statement Mr. Addy had made was handed up to him.

* Embracery: It dates back to 1470 and is the offense of influencing a jury illegally and corruptly.

Later on there was another interruption when the judge told the jurors: "Defense counsel is a little anxious about the matter to which Mr. Addy was so outrageously subject. I told you earlier that you will all dismiss the incident utterly from your minds as having no relation to the issue which you have to try. I thought I sufficiently conveyed to you by those words that there is no kind of evidence that the approaches were made on behalf of these accused men, or any particular accused man, and you will entirely dismiss the incident from your minds. It has no bearing on your task which is sufficiently difficult without it."

Two days later there was a sequel to the jury drama. The judge ordered the police to carry out a round-the-clock protection watch on the families of the jurors when they retired to consider their verdicts.

He said to the jury: "The Clerk of the Court tells me that in view of the incident involving Mr. Addy, you are all desirous to be assured that there can be no kind of interference with your families while you are in retirement. So far as it is within my power I direct the police authorities that protection will be provided for twenty-four hours of each day. It may be a matter of difficulty, for I know the police force is extended and taxed to an almost impossible extent, but that will be done I am sure."

There was to be another surprise during the judge's "back-breaking" summing-up which lasted through six days and more than a quarter of a million words. On

Day 46, Friday, March 20, the jury's hide-out was the topic. There had been keen speculation as to its whereabouts. Mr. Justice Davies took an opportunity to praise the Press in his soft lilting Welsh accent. At the same time he gave a warning. "I address no one in particular and there may be no substance in what I have been informed. But it has been brought to my attention that a reporter, not of the national Press, has indicated his intention of revealing the retiring place of the jury in this case. I am sure that it is undesirable that the retiring place of the jury be divulged. No pressman who desires to adhere to the high traditions of his honorable calling would do anything so inamicable to the public interest as that. The conduct of the Press during this long trial has been absolutely immaculate. They have, although the temptations must have been very great at times, disclosed nothing that ought not to have been disclosed. There have been occasions when the jury was in retirement that newsworthy matters have cropped up. The Press have been most loyal in the manner in which they have reported and not reported matters. I have no power in the matter at the moment. Maybe on reflection I will find I have power; but any reporter who for catch-penny reasons makes use of such information is doing something which will let down the high calling of the Press. And I hope the information I have is wholly erroneous and nothing of the kind is likely to occur."

Words which the twelve jurors must have relished

hinted that their daily excursions to the court were nearly over when Mr. Justice Davies said with a smile on Day 47 that his summing-up was nearly over.

He would leave a piece over for Monday, he said, and commented: "We will assemble here as usual at 10 a.m. You will each bring with you your night-cases. How long you will be in retirement I don't know but you must come fully prepared. That means everything you require you will bring with you. If I may embark on a homely topic—if you are smokers bring your smokes. If you are sweet-eaters bring your sweets. Nothing may be sent out for. You will have no wireless, no television, no newspapers. No messages can be delivered to you, either by note or 'phone, and in no way can you communicate with people outside. There have been cases in our legal history where it has been said that juries have improperly taken into their retirement documents which ought not to have been taken. You will be taking all the documents you are in receipt of, and I hope you will not mind, in case legal representatives want to examine them, making available for inspection your night-cases as well as your documents before you return. You will be completely incommunicado immediately you leave this court on Monday until you intimate to us that you are ready to return."

When the judge eventually reached the end of his marathon speech at 3 p.m. on the Monday (he had spoken for more than thirty hours) final orders went out to the jury, about to plough through the mass of evidence.

They were thanked for their "heroic attitude" during the forty-eight days so far. They departed with laughter echoing around the courtroom, for the foreman of the jury stated that he and his colleagues wished to have all the exhibits to examine—"all of them except the cash," he said briskly. Feelings of relief must have mingled with the laughter. The judge smiled. A wave of jollity spread through the dock, the Press tables, the well of the court and the public gallery.

The jurors left for their hiding place. The long wait had started.

They had been warned to inform the bailiffs not later than 5 p.m. on any one night if they had reached their verdicts. Reassembling the court would take at the least two hours, and the judge did not wish to sit at too late an hour.

The hours crept by. Twenty-four. Forty-eight. Then on the third night of their captivity came an inkling that verdicts had been agreed upon—at 9 p.m. on Wednesday, March 25. The jury wanted to return to the courtroom at ten the following morning.

It was in fact 10:30 a.m. on Thursday, March 26, when the jurors, pale and tired, returned to the packed courtroom—sixty-six hours and twenty-four minutes since retiring. It was the longest retirement of any jury in British legal history.

More than three hundred people were packed into the paneled court that morning. It was Day Number 51 of the trial.

One by one the accused trooped into the dock. First came Jim Hussey at 10:07 a.m., then Robert Welch. Behind them the other eight. Seated among them were burly prison officers. Police officers flanked the outside of the dock. In all forty-four police of all ranks could be counted in the well of the court, including Scotland Yard's chief detectives and leading police officials from Buckinghamshire.

Everyone waited tensely. At twenty-nine minutes past ten Mr. Justice Davies appeared, looking tireder than he had on that first morning so many days before.

The ten prisoners sat calmly, occasionally looking towards relatives in the public gallery.

Before the jury marched in, the judge spoke: "No one is to enter or leave this court until the proceedings are over. I want no stampede. But if the prison officers prefer to move each individual accused as his case is over, then that may most certainly be done."

Ten thirty . . . the entry of the jury. They looked heavy-eyed as they filed to their cordoned-off seats, carrying their boxes loaded with documents.

Ten thirty-two . . . the white-haired jury foreman stood erect.

"Are you agreed on your verdicts?"

"We are," he said nervously. Sometimes he had been inaudible.

Chubby-faced William Boal stood to attention.

"Do you find him guilty of being a robber or receiver? Just answer yes or no."

The jury foreman pondered. "Yes," he announced.

Boal, pale faced, was found guilty of conspiracy and armed robbery. He was also found guilty of robbing Frank Dewhurst of 120 mailbags. He was convicted of being a robber and conspirator.

The verdicts in respect of the others were: Charles Frederick Wilson: Guilty of being a robber and conspirator. Thomas John Wisbey: Guilty of being a robber and conspirator. Robert Welch: Guilty of being a robber and conspirator. James Hussey: Guilty of being a robber and conspirator. Roy James: Guilty of being a robber and conspirator. Douglas Gordon Goody: Guilty of being a robber and conspirator. Brian Field: Guilty of being a conspirator to rob. Guilty of conspiring with Leonard Field and John Wheater to conceal the identity of the purchaser of Leatherslade Farm and obstructing the course of public justice. Not guilty of being a robber. Not guilty of receiving £100,900 [$305,309].

Leonard Field was found guilty of being a conspirator to rob. Guilty of conspiring with Brian Field and John Wheater to conceal the identity of the purchaser of Leatherslade Farm and obstructing the course of public justice. Not guilty (on the judge's direction) of being a robber.

John Wheater, found guilty of conspiring with Brian Field and Leonard Field to conceal the identity of the purchaser of Leatherslade Farm and obstructing the course of public justice. Not guilty of being a conspirator to rob.

The jury was dismissed from returning verdicts against Boal and Roy James for receiving charges.

It was 10:42 a.m. It was all over.

Ten minutes had been long enough to convict the ten men of at least one of the charges they faced. An eleventh man, Roger John Cordrey, had pleaded guilty on the first day to conspiracy to rob, not guilty of robbery, and guilty to three charges of receiving.

The accused appeared unemotional. They received the verdicts calmly, with in some cases a shrug of the shoulder or a nervous twitch of the lips. Once or twice a sob could be heard in the public gallery.

Sentences, said the judge, would be held over until the remaining trials were held. These were to start on April 8.

Nearing the end of the first part of the trial, Mr. Justice Davies told the jury they had suffered an "unbearable burden over many weeks." He added: "Not only this county but the whole country is grateful to you. Your services are enormously appreciated."

He said they would be exempted from further jury service for the rest of their lives, and ended, "but a more worthy jury I cannot imagine."

Ripples of laughter echoed round the court when he added, "Life will never seem quite the same without you."

Facts and figures arising out of the trial were many. For instance, the fifty-one working days it took were spread over ten weeks. A mammoth two hundred and sixty-four witnesses gave evidence. Two million five hundred words were uttered. Mr. Justice Edmund Davies spoke for thirty-three hours. A team of six shorthand writers filled up thirty-four hundred-page notebooks. The jury examined six hundred and thirteen exhibits and were paid fifty shillings a day for their services. They listened to speeches by twenty-three barristers. And financially the trial is likely to have cost something in the region of one hundred thousand pounds.

But the Great Train Robbery trial will not go down in the records as the longest ever. The Tichborne case ninety years ago lasted one hundred and eighty days.

A twelfth man, Ronald Arthur Biggs, who at an earlier stage of the trial had been the subject of "an irregularity," faced a separate trial in the RDC offices on Wednesday, April 8. After the first day it was transferred to the town center to the traditional assize court. The trial lasted for six days.

Biggs pleaded not guilty to charges of robbery and conspiracy. He admitted he had been at Leatherslade Farm two days before the train raid. His prints were found on a Pyrex plate, the lid of a game of *Monopoly* and a bottle of tomato ketchup. He said he had gone there with a friend, Norman Bickers, on August 6. Biggs had been offered a part in "a big enterprise," but when he saw a large quantity of army uniforms at the farm he feared a raid was planned on an army depot and said he wanted nothing to do with it.

The next day Bickers found out there was to be a raid on the train and Biggs said they both pulled out and returned to London.

On the sixth day the jury of nine men and three women retired. After ninety minutes they returned to the court.

"Guilty on both charges," announced the jury foreman. Biggs was later to join the other eleven convicted men. The man Bickers never turned up to give evidence.

Judgment day, Thursday, April 16, 1964, arrived. The market town's ancient assize court dating back to 1774 was packed.

Tucked away in a corner was Jack Mills, driver of the Glasgow to Euston mail train. He and at least another two hundred and fifty people heard the judge say, when Cordrey groped his way into the dock: "You are the first to be sentenced out of eleven greedy men whom hope of gain allured. You and your co-conspirators have been convicted of complicity in one way or another, of a crime which in its impudence and enormity is the first of its kind in this country.

"I propose to do all in my power to ensure it will also be the last of its kind. Your outrageous conduct constitutes an intolerable menace to the well-being of society. Let us clear out of the way any romantic notions of dare-deviltry. This is nothing less than a sordid crime of violence inspired by vast greed. All who have seen that nerve-shattered engine driver can have no doubt of the terrifying effect on the law-abiding citizen of a concerted assault by armed robbers. To deal with this crime leniently would be a positively evil thing to do.

"When a grave crime is committed it calls for grave punishment, not for the purpose of mere retribution but that others similarly tempted will be brought to the realization that crime does not pay, and the game is not worth even the most alluring candle. Potential criminals who might be dazzled by the enormity of the prize must be taught that the punishment they risk must be pro-portionately greater.

"I therefore find myself faced with the unenviable task of pronouncing grave sentences. You and the other accused vary widely in intelligence, strength of person-ality and antecedent history. Some have absolutely clean characters up to the present. Some have previous con-victions of a comparatively minor character. Others have previous convictions of gravity which could lead to sentences of corrective training or preventive deten-tion. To some the degradation to which all of you have sunk now will bring consequences vastly more cruel than to others. Whatever the past of a particular accused, it pales into insignificance in the light of his present offenses.

"Furthermore, the evidence, or rather the lack of it,

renders it impossible to determine exactly what part was played by each of the eleven accused convicted of the larger conspiracy or the eight convicted of actual robbery. After mature deliberation, I propose to treat you all in the same manner, with two exceptions."

Cordrey was the first exception. The judge said he had admitted his guilt from the outset and his information had led to the police's finding nearly £80,000 [$224,-080].

His confession deserved recognition, said the judge.

He jailed Cordrey for twenty years on charges of conspiracy to rob and three charges of receiving. Gasps from the public gallery greeted this announcement. Then one by one the other accused stepped into the dock. And one by one the judge addressed them.

The eldest man on trial, William Boal, fifty, was next. The judge told him: "You have expressed no repentance for your wrongdoing. Instead, you continued to assert your innocence but you begged for mercy. Having seen you and heard you, I cannot believe you were one of the originators of the conspiracy or that you played a very dynamic part in it or the robbery itself."

Boal, guilty of conspiracy and robbery, was jailed for twenty-four years.

To Charles Wilson, another robber and conspirator, the judge said, "No one has said less than you throughout this long trial. I doubt if you have spoken half a dozen words and certainly no word of repentance has been expressed by you. If you or any of the other accused had assisted justice, that would have told strongly in your favor. The consequence of this vast booty of something like two and a half million pounds still remains entirely unrecovered. It would be an affront to the public if any one of you should be at liberty in anything like the near future to enjoy those ill-gotten gains."

Wilson got thirty years. The court was shocked into silence.

Accused number four was Ronald Biggs. He listened grim-faced to the words: "What I do know is that you are a specious and facile liar and have this week perjured yourself time and again." Again thirty years' prison for conspiracy and robbery.

Thirty years was Wisbey's punishment as he made a smart about-turn after the judge said, "You yourself have thrown no light on what part you played or any other topic. You have not sought to mollify the court by any repentance."

Handsome Robert Welch: thirty years for robbery and conspiracy.

Big Jim Hussey said, "Thank you, My Lord," for his thirty years' sentence for the same offenses.

Then diminutive Roy "The Weasel" James stood before the judge. "You are the only one of the accused in respect of whom it has been proved you actually received a substantial part of the stolen money. You still had £12,000 [$33,612] when you were arrested and I have

97

no doubt the original sum far exceeded that figure," said the judge. He added, "In a short space of time you had what your counsel described as a brilliant and meteoric success as a racing driver. I strongly suspect it was your known talent as a driver which enabled you to play an important part in the perpetration of this grave crime."

For James: thirty years.

Broad-shouldered Douglas Gordon Goody was next. The judge's analysis was, "In some respects you present this court with one of the saddest problems by which it is confronted in this trial. You have manifest gifts of personality and intelligence which could have carried you far had they been directed honestly. I have not seen you in the court for three months without noticing that you are a man capable of inspiring the admiration of your fellow accused."

Goody, called by the judge "a dangerous menace to society," was given thirty years.

To Brian Field the judge said, "Your strength of personality and superior intelligence enabled you to obtain a position of dominance in relation to your employer John Wheater. I entertain no serious doubts that you are in no small measure responsible for the disastrous position in which this wretched man now finds himself. That you played an essential role in the major conspiracy is clear." His sentence was twenty-five years.

The judge called Leonard Field "a dangerous man." And his seventy-three-year-old mother up in the public gallery produced the only signs of emotion during the trial. She shouted, "He's innocent! I'm his old mother. Justice is not right."

Mrs. Field had to be ejected from the court, as her son turned and said: "Don't worry, mum. I'm still young."

He got twenty-five years.

To the last convicted man, John Denby Wheater, the judge said, "You have served your country gallantly in war and faithfully in peace. There is no evidence that you contributed to your present position by profligate living of any kind. Indeed, your standards seem to have been distinctively lower than your managing clerks."

Wheater went to prison for three years, and the judge's task was almost over.

Still remaining were minor trials against seven people accused of receiving. They were finished over the next two days.

Alfred Pilgrim, his wife Florence, and Mrs. Rene Boal were cleared of receiving £860 [$2,408.80], and Mrs. Boal a further £330 [$924.33]. They all pleaded not guilty.

William Pelham, twenty-six, a mechanic who admitted receiving £545 [$1,527.54], was given a conditional discharge.

Walter Albert Smith was jailed for three years for receiving £2,000 [$5,602], which he admitted. His wife Patricia denied receiving £450 [$1,260.45] and was acquitted.

99

Finally Martin Harvey, a driver, admitted receiving £518 [$1,450.91] and went to prison for twelve months.

Reactions to the judge's heavy sentences were instant and varied. In general it was felt that they were too severe. As the *Daily Mail* wrote in an editorial, "People everywhere are puzzled by one glaring contrast. It is this —an evildoer convicted of conspiracy and robbery as in the Train Case can be sentenced to thirty years which, with normal remission, means serving twenty years in prison. But an evildoer convicted of murder and jailed for life is unlikely to serve more than fifteen years.

"Does this mean that stealing banknotes is regarded as being more wicked than murdering somebody? What is the real purpose of punishment in both cases? To mete out retribution? To deter others? To reform the criminal?"

James Cameron, writing in *The Daily Herald*, pointed out that those of the gang sentenced would have got lighter sentences for non-capital murder, still lighter for blackmail, infinitely lighter for breaking a baby's legs. Our legal system tended to take a sterner view of crimes against property than crimes against people. "Two million pounds was a tremendous lot of property," he added dryly.

The Daily Telegraph denied it could necessarily be inferred that the law values property more highly than life. "Another interpretation is that killers are thought less susceptible to deterence than thieves—a view main-

100

tained by many experts of crime," it declared in its main leader on the day after the sentences. "Certainly the learned judge made it clear that his severity aimed at striking fear into the heart of the criminal world by making the penalty match the exorbitance of the offense."

The Guardian described the sentences as "out of proportion with everything except the value of the property involved."

Competing on front pages with the sentences was a story about a Parliamentary committee which had found that the electronics firm of Ferranti had made an unfair profit of more than £4-million [$11,204,000] from a Government missile contract. This situation was succinctly summed up by Belsky in a cartoon in the *Daily Herald*. It showed a father telling his son after reading the newspaper, "Well, that shows crime doesn't pay. Government missiles—that's what you want to go in for."

7

THEORY AND SPECULATION: THE PLANNING

The two mighty mysteries of the great train robbery—who planned it and where the main booty is—remain unsolved.

The chronicle of the crime so far set down in these pages has dealt with known factual elements—the deed itself, the discovery of the hideout and the trial of certain accused persons.

We come now to the realm of theory and speculation in probing the unknown factors and here our scope ranges from the romantic to the fantastic.

Newspaper sleuths assigned to the case have come up with a variety of guesses at the identity of the mastermind behind the coup, and one specialist team plumped boldly for "The Major," not to be confused with a fence and petty crook who revels in a similar pseudonym.

This one is said to have been an officer in the Army and his timing of the raid was taken to indicate Commando training. He left Army issue trenching tools behind him at the first hide-out.

An Irishman believed to have led three big bank raids in Dublin was favored by another crime reporter. The police were said to have shadowed a baronet who was known to have underworld associates. They even attended his Mayfair parties in the course of their duties.

Robert Traini of the *Daily Herald* was convinced that the robbery was not the scheme of a single mastermind but had been worked out by five men who shortly after the raid fled abroad, probably to South America, with their wives.

In his story of how the police almost captured Bruce Reynolds, Anthony Lejeune described him as "the principal planner." The police, according to the prosecution in the opening stages of the trial, believed that there was no single "master mind."

In the opinion of ex-Detective-Superintendent Gosling, each of these theories contains some truth. Of the gang of fifteen, five whose names are known, including Reynolds, played major roles in the planning. An Irishman is known to have been one of the principals but there is insufficient evidence for the Crown to gain a conviction.

The story that got nearest the truth is the one about "The Major" but it was mistaken both in the *nom de guerre* of the ex-Army officer and also in saying that police knew his name and record. There are no fingerprints or photographs on police files of this wartime hero, who, incidentally, was never referred to by the train robbers by any name other than Johnnie Rainbow.

The story of this man, who for legal reasons can be referred to only by his code name, has been carefully built up by Gosling during the months since the robbery. It can—and undoubtedly will—be challenged by many of those who have worked on the case as investigators, lawyers or reporters.

The co-author has however been in a unique position. In his days as head of the Ghost Squad his reputation for possessing the most lucrative list of informers of any officer at Scotland Yard was unrivaled. In fact when he retired in 1957 one of the top men who worked on the train robbery case offered Gosling a substantial sum of money for his personal file containing the names, aliases, addresses and telephone numbers of his personal "snouts."

Gosling's reply was typical.

"You can have the lot for nothing, lad—but it won't do you any good."

His informers had one thing in common. They hated all coppers—with one exception. In more than thirty years of crime detection Gosling established himself more as a friend than an enemy. He was known as a man of compassion, a freebooter who knew when to be as relentlessly authoritarian as Victor Hugo's gendarme Javert and when to turn a Nelson's eye. They dubbed him "The Yokel," a nickname which reflected his massive build and ruddy complexion and not any slowness of wit. And since he retired to an 18th-century farmhouse in the Olde Worlde atmosphere of Brantham in Suffolk, men and women who have spent more years in prison than out have looked him up. Some wanted to demonstrate that even the most hardened criminal can go straight, but the majority are recidivists who call on him purely for the sake of auld lang syne.

The word spread quickly via the grapevine that Gosling wanted information on the Great Train Robbery in his unofficial capacity as a retired detective turned crime writer. He is convinced that, thanks to one of his underworld friends, he actually discussed the robbery on the telephone with the master-mind, Johnnie Rainbow. The conversation was probably not conclusive enough to take the case any farther forward so far as the official investigation was concerned. Even so, when Gosling tried to see his former junior, who worked on the case, he could not get an interview. "He's too busy on the case," he was told.

In the light of what follows, this may appear to most readers to have been unfortunate.

Johnnie Rainbow was once one of the most dedicated officers in the British Regular Army. He joined as a boy soldier in 1938 straight from one of Scotland's bleakest, grimmest orphanages. Parentless and homeless, the Army immediately became everything to him. For most of the other lads who joined with him the break from home, the grinding discipline, the senseless restrictions were purgatory. But for Johnnie, King and Country really meant something.

He followed his dream through the African desert, occupied Europe, Palestine, Korea, Egypt and Cyprus— years of excitement and action in which he won a Military Medal in France and a Military Cross as a "peacetime" officer in one of many post-war campaigns.

It was the sheer boredom of garrison life in England which got him in the end. That was when he started to go racing. Where others dabbled, he plunged. It was bad luck that just about this time he was put in charge of regimental funds and within six months the Army auditors caught up with him.

The last-minute miracle he hoped for never happened. His unblemished record, years of service, the way his old commanding officer spoke up for him, counted for nothing in the end. He walked out of Command Headquarters for the last time in 1957 after a court-martial which stripped him of his honor and his identity. The next few months in the life of this strongly-built, fair-headed Scot with an accent which years of travel had neutralized are a mystery. But in 1958 he turned up in London where his constant companion for several months was Fred Hankie, a garage owner. Fred, a lean, lantern-jawed Cockney character, has an early record of crime but for many years now he has been officially "clean." An expert mechanic, he served with Johnnie in the desert when both were sergeants and one of those inexplicable but lasting friendships was struck between this ill-assorted couple—the indoctrinated, super-military officer from the ranks and the former tearaway.

After leaving the Army Fred started his own business, a small garage, with what were undoubtedly the best intentions. But almost inevitably his workshop soon became a place where the engine number of a stolen car and a new set of plates could be changed, a car hotted up for a quick getaway or so transformed that the real owner would not recognize it.

Johnnie lived on the charity of his old sergeant for several weeks. His problems were crushing him and he relied on the bottle more and more. In the shrewd way of criminals, Fred realized his old officer's real worth both as a leader and as the physically toughest man he had ever encountered. With his training Johnnie would make a superb underworld operator if he could be introduced into the right circles without completely shedding his dignity and illusions. He was already convinced that with his background and military record, the world owed him a living.

It was Fred or one of his associates who introduced Johnnie to one of the post-war phenomena of organized crime, Dingo Harry. Various people have laid claim to the title of "King of the Underworld" but, as even the rawest recruit on the Metropolitan beat knew, the Dingo had not had a serious rival for many years.

This Australian, who was reputed to be so strong that he could crack walnuts between his thumb and index finger and so quick with a razor that he was sometimes called "The Head Surgeon," was operating roulette and chemin-de-fer games in London. The Act which has legalized certain gaming was then a matter of academic discussion. Harry successfully evaded the law by renting a different house or apartment each night. The address was revealed to a selected group of addicts who included a fantastic cross-section of moneyed aristocrats, businessmen and criminals.

The strong-arm boys normally employed by Dingo Harry had proved an embarrassment. They could neither mix socially with such a clientele nor, on the rare but inevitable occasions when there was trouble and force was necessary, could they handle it discreetly. The cashiered officer with his acquired air of elegance and breeding, ready supply of small talk and Commando-trained ferocity, was exactly right.

In the three years that he looked after the gambling club interests of Dingo Harry, Johnnie got to know every villain of any note in London. For their part, they respected him as a man with "class" who, although in a sense one of themselves, kept his hands clean. All he could ever have been arrested for was a technical breach of the gaming laws which meant a fine and nothing more.

The underworld's respect for him was not returned by Johnnie. It seemed to him when he listened to their past triumphs and future plans that most of them had spent more time in prison than out. Often he would cut in on some reminiscence of a botched or semi-successful job and ask why the thief had not taken more time, or point out some defect that seemed to him obvious. He was constantly amazed by the lack of care which tripped up those who were caught—the badly-stitched buttons which came off, the rubber gloves carelessly left at home, the identifiable footprint deposited neatly on the pathway. And most of them talked too much.

But there were exceptions—exceptions like Bruce Reynolds and Douglas Gordon Goody. As a young man, Reynolds had worked as a bookmaker's clerk but he had always been on the fringes of crime. In his early twenties he abandoned his job to become a full-time villain. Reynolds had made a study of antiques and, using the small antique shop he opened in South London as a front, he began a flourishing practice in crime. He was able to take up motor racing, fly to the South of France to play the casino tables and generally live a life which set him apart from the usual run of criminal. Goody had been a criminal from his childhood days during the war when he led a gang of East End boys and girls who plundered bombed homes. Gradually he graduated into the big time and although he was convicted several times as a young man, with more experience he acquired the reputation of being an "alibi king." On several occasions the police were positive that they had him for various crimes, but he was always able to prove that he was somewhere else when the crimes were committed.

These were the only types of men, Johnnie decided, he would trust if he were actively engaged in crime. But he had no such plans. He enjoyed his work, rubbing shoulders with people from all worlds. They all seemed to accept him as one of themselves. He dealt with trouble tactfully or ruthlessly as the situation demanded. On the few occasions that he had to call on those who had passed dud checks but who were too important to be dealt with by Harry's tearaways, his cold blue eyes and the hidden threat in his calmly authoritative manner worked wonders. The money was always forthcoming and there were no repercussions with the law.

It became obvious in 1960 that legalized gambling would soon be introduced to Britain, and Johnnie was given a new job in the gang leader's empire. He was sent to Tangier to control his smuggling operations.

This was work he really enjoyed. The sunshine, the days on the beach and the occasional voyage with the smugglers—in direct contradiction of his orders from Harry to expose himself as little as possible—were a welcome contrast after two unbroken years of night life.

After only eighteen months in Tangier, however, Johnnie returned to London. He would not talk about his reasons for leaving North Africa while Dingo Harry made it plain to one and all that even to mention Johnnie's name when he was around was asking for trouble. It was said there had been a quarrel between the two because the ex-officer had refused to have anything to do with drug smuggling. But this is unlikely, for the Australian had always let it be known that no matter what the profits might be and how bad his record, he would never touch the dope trade.

Whatever the reasons in 1961 Johnnie was back in London, living comfortably off the money he had saved and apparently in no hurry to get back to work of any description. He avoided all but a chosen few of his underworld associates. Whether it was his idea to plan the robbery of the August Bank Holiday train from Scotland or whether his associates persuaded him to lead them is a matter for speculation.

The possibilities of robbing the mail train were first discussed in Wormwood Scrubs. An ex-railwayman who was serving time there frequently spoke of the ease with which it could be done. He described how the train left Glasgow with clockwork regularity each night; how the money and valuables were always carried in the first two coaches containing unarmed sorters. Two of the prisoners who were serving sentences for burglary soon saw the possibilities of bringing off the great coup of all time. It would, they agreed, need the most careful precision planning and, above all, organization. As run-of-the-mill and fairly unsuccessful criminals they were under no illusions about their own capacities to stage-manage such a job.

They agreed to put their information before the smartest and coolest operators they knew in the underworld, Bruce Reynolds and Goody. When they were released early in 1962 they went to Reynolds. He was immediately enthusiastic. The two ex-prisoners tried to talk him into forming a gang immediately so that they could rob the Glasgow-London mail train carrying the 1962 August bank holiday bonanza. With the prospect of so much money—anything up to £8-million [$22,408,-000], the ex-railwayman had assured him—so quickly, Reynolds was tempted. So was Goody but they needed another opinion outside their normal circle of acquaintances who, in the reckless way of criminals the world over, would all be greedy for immediate action. The hardened criminal's philosophy is rarely understood by ordinary people who, if they have ever entertained

112

dishonest ideas, are deterred by thoughts of the law's retribution. The recidivist will cheerfully face the prospect of years behind bars for the excitement and short-lived rewards of a profitable piece of larceny.

So they sought out the one man they know who was "straight," with an unblemished record—yet who at the same time was trusted and respected by the underworld. Johnnie, who was leading the life of a man of means, was fascinated by the scale of the operation. He pointed out the danger of rushing such a job. It would require split-second timing. The gang would have to be trained to act silently, efficiently and, if necessary, ruthlessly. They would have to plan with the help of someone who knew how the railway system worked, preferably a man who could drive a train. And had they thought what they would do with so much money?

At some stage in these talks Johnnie became established as the brains of the robbery. A mind such as his, trained both for action and minute detail, was essential for its success, and Reynolds and Goody gladly recognized him as leader. All thoughts of staging the robbery in 1962 were abandoned when it was realized that the ex-railwayman who was to play such a vital role would not be released from "The Scrubs" until the winter.

It was agreed that it would be best to wait. It would give them time to recruit the most dependable, professional men they knew, men who could be relied upon not to talk before or after.

The biggest obstacle of all, Johnnie pointed out, was the ready money needed to set up such a coup. They must have cash to buy a hide-out large enough and sufficiently remote for the gang to lie low at until the initial heat was off them. A fleet of fast, utterly reliable vehicles for transporting the loot and making a quick getaway was vital. And they must be certain that, having hand-picked the best men for the job, there would be no danger of their pulling off bits of private enterprise in the meantime which might put them behind bars and out of action for the train raid.

The only way to ensure that members of the gang would go straight until needed for the train robbery was to see they had sufficient money until then to live comfortably without financial worries. The two men agreed that the most effective way would be to pull off a less ambitious job to finance their enterprise. They decided that the best way to get unmarked money in sufficient quantity with a fair chance of getting away would be a wages raid.

By now Reynolds had recruited seven other top operators who were taken completely into their confidence so that they would work as a team. It was one of these who suggested London Airport as the best target. He had inside knowledge of the system and had for some time tried to work out a plan for grabbing the large weekly pay packet.

If any of the gang doubted Johnnie's capabilities at

the beginning, the way he planned this job eliminated them for all time. For several Fridays he watched the guards take the money from Barclay's Bank to Comet House at London Airport, a distance of 200 yards. Their timetable was unvarying, so that he could stopwatch it almost to a second. The routine of loading it on a trolley outside Comet House and taking it by elevator to the top floor was always the same. He conceived the plan of concealing men in an upper floor of the building who would come down in the elevator when the security men summoned it and take them by surprise.

His final touch was to make them dress in the uniform of city businessmen, complete with black bowler hats and furled umbrellas. As a uniform—any uniform—is a symbol of authority in some countries, the outfit of a "city gent" in England is one of respectability.

Perhaps to prove to the gang that he was no back-room general who was not prepared to take risks, Johnnie led the airport raid. It went off exactly as planned and their disguise was good enough for them all to get away unidentified except one man who was later convicted. It yielded £62,500 [$175,062.50].

Each man was given £4,000 [$11,204] to tide him over until the following August, nine months ahead, while the remaining £22,500 [$63,022.50] was kept in reserve to finance the big robbery and for further retainers to new recruits. They would need more men, who could be brought in later, for any strong-arm stuff which might be required in quelling the train's sorters and guards and to transfer the money rapidly to the waiting vehicles. Such men are referred to with some contempt by both criminals and police as "laborers."

One of the most important members of the gang, an expert transport officer who could ensure that the get-away vehicles were in perfect condition and who could, if the ultimate plan misfired, drive off with what was left of the loot and the gang and shake off any pursuers, was recruited early on. It sounded just the job to Roy James, the brilliant young racing motorist who had been mixed up in crime from boyhood, and the handsome retainer he was paid gave him the chance meanwhile to indulge his love of racing.

The first hint of dissent and challenge to Johnnie's leadership came when it was time to recruit someone who could deal with the signals. They found the perfect man, a former electrician who had become an expert technician in many fields. He had played a vital role in two previous train hold-ups and knew the railway signaling system as well as any full-time employee of British Railways.

"Tippler," as he was known because of his drinking habits, was enthusiastic about the job. He admired the way it was being handled in the preliminary stages but he would not accept the terms of the two leaders who told him that his share would be a straight £50,000. He insisted that every member of the gang should be paid an equal share, no matter what his role. If the train carried as much money as anticipated, every man's share would be enough to last him the rest of his life. But if some were given less than others there would be the temptation to "grass"—especially if the reward money was considerably more than their share.

If there were equal shares, he reasoned, there would be no grounds for resentment. After long arguments the Tippler agreed to a compromise. Each member of the gang would receive an equal share except Johnnie and Reynolds who, he acknowledged, as the planners and organizers should each get a double share.

The technician agreed to recruit the "laborers," all men who had worked for him on his own criminal enterprises, who trusted him and who could be relied upon to act efficiently and ruthlessly if necessary.

The final strength of the gang, it was agreed, should be seventeen, but there was no need to start rehearsing them until three months before the raid took place in August. In the meantime, however, there was much detail to be attended to by the two planners.

The 6:50 p.m. mail train from Glasgow to London was checked and re-checked for four weeks at various places along the line to see how closely it followed its scheduled timetable, and what action was taken if it ran late. After Sears Crossing was finally chosen as the raiding spot, because of its remoteness combined with its proximity to the end of the journey when all the money would be in the high-value coach, the search began for a hide-out.

The search and negotiations were left to Brian Field. Field, who was married to a German woman, worked for John Denby Wheater, a criminal lawyer who had appeared for the defense in the trial which followed the London Airport raid. The lawyer and his future clerk met when they served in the Army, Wheater as an officer in the judiciary department, Field as a corporal clerk in the same unit. Wheater was later implicated in the train robbery but his was a passive role and he was never a member of the gang.

Reynolds, whose hobbies included cine-photography, filmed the mobile Post Office on a number of occasions as it passed over Bridego Bridge. He also took movies of the surrounding terrain so that the gang would be familiar with the area without ever "casing" it themselves.

Reynolds's subsequent film was shown and re-shown to members of the gang in a basement club which became the gang's regular meeting place. The timing of the operation and what each man's job was to be were drummed into the gang once they had been fully and finally selected.

The ex-railwayman who had first mooted the robbery in prison was one of the last to be recruited. Johnnie insisted that every man must become not only familiar with the task of uncoupling a train but so expert that he could do it in the dark without even a torch to aid him. So, in ones and twos, they went to "night school" at various railway sidings around London with their "tutor."

By the first week in August every member of the gang knew his station and his role. Leatherslade Farm had been acquired and the Weasel knew to within seconds how long the journey with the loot and the gang would take from the bridge. The farmhouse had been stocked with enough food and drink for a stay of two weeks and Tippler had installed short-wave radio. He set this on the County Police's wavelength so that they would be able to follow progress of the search. Walkie-talkie sets were also brought so that communication could be maintained between the first wave, who were to hijack the engine and high-value coaches, and the "shock troops" at Sears Crossing whose job it was to overpower the sorters.

Throughout the planning of the raid there had been harmony at all levels once the question of the share-out had been settled. But the ultimate disposal of the money proved the biggest obstacle.

Johnnie could not dictate what each man should do with his share but he put forward a plan which to him, and several others, seemed watertight for the almost immediate disappearance of the entire haul. If all the gang had fallen in with his scheme most of them would have been able to return to their homes immediately after the money had been counted.

But about half the gang—including Tippler—insisted on a pay-out so that they could handle their own shares.

Where money was concerned, they trusted nobody and preferred to take their chances on the run to pooling the proceeds and letting Johnnie and Reynolds control their loot.

THEORY AND
SPECULATION:
THE LOOT

8

As bookmaker Charles Wilson warned the police when they arrested him, "I don't see how you can make it stick without the poppy and you won't find that." After the initial discoveries of money at Bournemouth, in the woods near Dorking and in the Whites' caravan, the police and insurance assessors were confident that before long they would recover most or all of the stolen

121

money. It seemed at that stage that in their haste to rid themselves of their embarrassment of riches, the gang were simply throwing the money away.

But the bulk of the "poppy" is still missing. Whatever evidence the police had and no matter how well founded their suspicions, these have been largely negated by the absence of the only real proof—the missing millions. They followed their usual routine of watching for signs of free spending among their suspects before arrest, a vanity which has given away countless criminals. One classic dodge for getting rid of hot money is for a criminal to arrange a big "win" through a crooked bookmaker who gives clean money at a discount in exchange for stolen notes. So betting shops were combed and their books examined for evidence of unusually big coups.

Eventually the police had to face it. Somehow £2,300,-000 weighing about 1¾ tons had disappeared without trace. How could it have been got rid of without attracting attention? The immensity of the haul was illustrated by the fact that it took six hours to count the £101,000 found near Dorking while it took two sacks to contain the £50,000 planted in a telephone kiosk. It also seemed impossible that such a vast hoard of notes could have been hidden for distribution at a later date.

Travelers to the Continent for many months after the inquiry were given some idea of how far Interpol was ranging in their inquiries. They brought back stories of waiting for several minutes at banks throughout Europe while English £5 notes they handed across to be changed were checked with lists of serial numbers.

Those who knew a little about banking and commerce theorized on the possibility of the money going to Swiss banks, but as the City staff of *The Times* pointed out in a clinical survey of possibilities, it would be difficult to get rid of the hoard anywhere in Europe.

"As far as Europe is concerned the Swiss banks are without doubt the most genuinely free-thinking establishments of their kind," the article stated. "Yet it is doubtful whether today any one of the leading institutions would readily accept, say, anything more than £1,000 in notes.

"Some, it is thought, might not shrink at £5,000, but even such an amount would at once arouse suspicion, and certainly now, so long after the actual theft and all the publicity it has received the world over. Smaller amounts, on the other hand, say bundles of £100 or £200, exchanged judiciously, would not present much of a problem. . . .

"Certainly anything like £1-million or more in notes offered suddenly anywhere on the Continent would have an immediate impact on the note rate even if such an amount is small in relation to genuine dealings on the foreign exchange market which run into many millions a day but are largely done on the telegraphic transfer system. In fact, a once-and-for-all exchange of a large amount of sterling notes is not thought to be a practical proposition on the Continent. . . .

"Another possible way toward quick exchange could lead via the gambling halls of Europe. Quite large amounts, say at least £1,000 at a time, might be quite readily acceptable in the big casinos of Cannes, Monte Carlo, Le Touquet and Baden-Baden.

"The cash would be changed into chips; if the gangster is lucky he will double his money with a coup or two and walk out with twice as much in the native currency. But the casinos know their large gamblers, and really big amounts exchanged by anyone not known as a habitué would arouse suspicion. Indeed, even if some members of the gang were able to exchange large amounts they would continue to attract suspicion. There is no easy way out, it seems, except for the robbers to sit on their hoard and use the money or exchange it only as required for normal living—*pace* C.I.D. or Scotland Yard."

The Guardian announced categorically that the numbers of more than half the stolen banknotes were known to the police who had circulated lists throughout the country. This statement, presumably inspired by one of the police officers on the case, was wildly inaccurate. The only numbers the banks were able to give the police were those of 15,000 £5 notes.

No full record of the numbers of £5 notes is kept, but the banks traditionally write down before despatch the numbers of two notes, selected at random, from each bundle.

Tips about "hot" fivers being sold at half price came in from informers to both the police and the insurance assessors, mainly to the latter, but arrests could be made only if people were found in possession of at least one of the 15,000 notes whose serial numbers were known.

The newspapers continued to report that the police were confident the money was hidden in London and were concentrating their search around the city in the hopes of finding it before the gangsters had a chance to make a final share-out.

Robert Traini on the other hand was sure that at the time *The Times* had the Flying Squad combing London, the loot was being successfully smuggled out of the country.

"The money was split up and taken to the Continent by five crooks who were the brains behind the robbery," he announced. "Detectives now know the £2,600,000 ambush of the Glasgow-Euston mail train at Cheddington was not the scheme of a single mastermind. The five planners sat down together in a South London club and drew up their blueprint for robbing the train. They worked on information from a former railway worker.

"Now the five have fled abroad, some with their wives. They plan to live in Europe or South America on the proceeds of the raid. Almost certainly they have changed their names and appearances and are buying property where they can settle like rich British businessmen. They have contacts on the Continent and are used to spending big money.

"These men like to live fast and furiously. But Scotland Yard expect them to lie low for a while in their surroundings. Two men named by Scotland Yard are now believed to have gone to Germany or Austria to have their faces changed by plastic surgery. . . ."

A report which came in from two fishermen, Peter Gilson—coxswain of the Southend lifeboat—and Arthur Plappert, sent police racing to the Thames Estuary in September in the belief that they were hot on the trail of the missing loot. The fishermen said that while in their longshore trawler near a group of seven small forts built during the war for anti-aircraft defense, they saw a cabin cruiser anchor nearby, beneath some gun emplacements.

"It was a really classy cruiser with glass windows all the way round," they reported to the police. "It wasn't flying any flag, but had two rags at the masthead which seemed to be some kind of distress signal. They weren't fishing or anything, which surprised us. We went for a closer look."

Five of the eight men in the cruiser were neatly dressed in collars and ties while the others looked as if they had not washed for weeks. Gilson asked if they needed help, but was told that everything was all right.

When a team of police and detectives arrived there was no sign of either the men or the cruiser, but it was thought that the forts might have made a good hiding place for money. However, nothing was found in them, nor in the muddy waters below which were searched by frogmen.

126

Among the boats watched by the police during their search for the loot was a five-ton motor yacht, *Christine*, which was owned by a thirty-year-old garage proprietor, Edward Anderson.

When the *Christine* was reported missing at sea on January 3 after sailing from Ramsgate, there was immediate speculation that its disappearance had something to do with the train robbery money.

Anderson had sailed his boat down the Thames in December—four months after the train robbery—to Margate where he discovered that it was shipping water badly. He left it with Mr. John Halmes, a marine engineer who took it to Ramsgate for temporary repairs. When Anderson told them he intended to sail *Christine* to Thames Ditton for major repairs Mr. Halmes begged him not to and was so worried when Anderson insisted on sailing, that he loaned him a big barge motor pump.

Helicopters, planes and a lifeboat scoured the seas off the south-east coast but the only trace of the *Christine* found was an empty rubber dinghy tied to a buoy seven miles north-east of the Foreland. Relays of frogmen also searched the area without success.

Three weeks later Anderson was found by *Daily Express* reporters in Dublin. At that stage, all he would say was that he had not sailed with the *Christine* but that his friend Dennis Bassett, aged thirty-three, had gone to sea in her with two other men.

Shortly after Anderson's dramatic reappearance Bassett's body was washed up off the Belgian coast. It was identified and brought back to England where a protracted inquest was held.

Anderson had hinted in newspaper interviews ever since coming out of hiding that the whole mystery surrounding the disappearance of the *Christine* and the reason why he fled to Ireland instead of sailing aboard her was connected with the train robbery. The police placed little credence on his vague statements that he had not liked the look of two of his passengers and had left the yacht because of a strange foreboding of disaster.

On March 1, however, Ken Gardner of *The People* printed a full statement made by Anderson that the *Christine* was carrying two of the train robbers and £1-million in notes. The newspaper considered the story so important that it led the front page, taking precedence over the Innsbruck air disaster of the previous day in which eighty-three Britons were killed.

Anderson, wrote Gardner, had broken his silence largely because he was in fear of his life. He felt he needed police protection.

"I am dead scared that my fate will be the same as Danny Bassett's," he said. "I know too much."

Anderson claimed that a few days after Christmas a friend phoned and asked to see him urgently. When they met he asked Anderson if he would like to earn £5,000 by taking a few parcels over to France. The *Christine* was to slip across the Channel and rendezvous off the coast

128

with another boat which would take the parcels. Anderson said he agreed after he had been assured the parcels did not contain drugs.

He was then told that as part of the deal he would have to take two passengers who would bring the parcels and transfer with them to the other boat eight miles off Dunkirk. After various delays for repairs to the *Christine*, he fixed the sailing day for January 2.

Anderson said that shortly after eleven o'clock that night a man came aboard carrying two heavy suitcases. A few minutes later when Anderson, Bassett and the stranger were drinking in the saloon, a second man arrived aboard. He was carrying a large brown canvas holdall.

Anderson at once recognized him as one of the men wanted by the police for the train robbery.

The newspaper report continued: "The man said, 'I suppose you know all about it, Eddie. I'll be glad when all this is over and done with.' He said that his wife was 'on the other side' and indicated that a car would be waiting to take him to her when he landed in France at dawn.

"All four men then went to the wheelhouse to study the charts and to give the engine a final inspection. Suddenly the second man to arrive nodded to Anderson to follow him to the saloon. There he said, 'You know what the arrangements are, Eddie. You'll be paid when we see the other boat.' That had been arranged for 3:30 a.m.

"Anderson asked if he had the money. The man replied by bending down and snapping open the fasteners on one of the suitcases. The lid flew back to reveal a case tightly packed with five-pound notes.

"Anderson asked if the other bags were also packed with notes. The man replied: 'What do you think?' The man grabbed several bundles of the fivers and said, 'This is for you, Eddie. Get us to the other side and it's yours.'

"At this point Anderson realized that he was being asked to carry some of the mail train loot. He was frightened. And he feared, too, the man who had waved the five-pound notes under his nose. This was a man who would know how to deal with awkward witnesses."

Anderson, who repeated his story the same night on television, said he walked back to the wheelhouse and told Bassett what he had seen. Bassett told him, "We're carrying a million quid in there from the train job."

Anderson said he was scared and told Bassett that he did not like it. Someone should have told him what the job entailed. Bassett replied that it was too late to quit now as they were sailing in a few minutes.

"Anderson made a sudden decision to quit," Ken Gardner reported. " 'Well, I'm not coming with you,' he said to Bassett. Then he grabbed his holdall of personal belongings and jumped from the yacht on to the quay. Bassett and the others shouted after him but nobody attempted to follow."

Said Anderson: "That was the last I saw of my yacht the *Christine*. I left Ramsgate in a blind panic. I could not think straight. Next day I caught a train to Birmingham and then took an aeroplane to Dublin."

When he returned from Dublin he had been afraid to tell the police about the money or the passenger he recognized. He was still afraid as he had received several phone calls warning him not to disclose the purpose of *Christine*'s voyage. He now felt it best to make a complete disclosure to the police.

The authors are as sceptical of Anderson's story as are the police. The flaws in it are obvious to the most casual reader.

In a TV appearance the next day Anderson repeated his account of why and how he disappeared. To most people it seemed a plausible story and it answered the all-important question of how a large part of the loot had disappeared.

The police were by no means convinced that his story held together. Why, they wondered, had Edwards suffered a sudden bout of conscience at the last moment. And how could two men have carried £1-million worth of notes aboard in two suitcases? Even if the money had all been in fivers, it would, they estimated, have weighed between 400 and 500 lb. and numerous cases would have been needed to hold it all. And they had discovered that Anderson's life had been insured by his business associate, Ronald Verrier, for £150,000.

When the inquest on Bassett began at Dover, Anderson gave a more detailed account. He claimed that the passenger he recognized as being on of the men wanted in connection with the train robbery was Ronald "Buster" Edwards.

"I recognized him straight away," he told the Coroner. "I have met him in the past. He was wearing dark glasses as a disguise and he had lost a lot of weight. He went below and Bassett poured him a drink. Edwards told me, 'You know what it's all about Eddie. We are the package.' "

Anderson described how Edwards opened one of the suitcases and produced a large wad of notes, mostly in £5 notes. But when the Coroner asked him if Edwards had told him some of the money was for him, he refused to answer on the grounds that he might incriminate himself.

It was fast becoming obvious that the Coroner was not impressed by his story. When Anderson described how he picked up his overnight bag just as the *Christine* was leaving and jumped overboard, the Coroner remarked, "It showed a remarkable presence of mind." He made another wry comment when Anderson accounted for his movements after leaving the boat.

"I hitched a lift to Margate and then phoned my father to drive down to pick me up," he said. "While waiting for him to arrive I slept below one of the arches of a railway bridge."

"Your worries did not keep you awake?" asked the Coroner.

Anderson said, "I was rather exhausted."

132

"I should have thought you had had the most exciting night of your life," the Coroner commented. "I am surprised to hear you slept that night." The Coroner twice asked Anderson if he really wished to stand by his story. Anderson said he did. He had jumped off the *Christine* because he feared he would be murdered. He was to have been the "fall guy."

"I thought the end product in this case would be the disappearance of Edwards and the other man on the *Christine* and the million pounds. I feared I might be eliminated because I knew too much and I had the pretty heavy insurance of £150,000 on my head, for which Verrier had paid the premium."

He denied that he went to sea on the *Christine* but was landed somewhere while Bassett was left aboard to be rescued later. "Ludicrous and out of the question," he said as if astonished at the very idea.

But at the resumed hearing a week later Anderson's counsel, Mr. John Lloyd-Eley, said that Anderson had reconsidered his position and wished to say that the account he had given on oath was untrue.

Anderson's revised version turned out to be even more sensational than his original story and caused the Coroner to remark: "We are getting more fantastic as we go along."

"Verrier wanted me to sail in the *Christine* and there was something about me falling overboard and drowning," Anderson stated. "A boat was to have picked me up on the Spanish or French coast so that Verrier could claim the £150,000 insurance. I would have had £30,000, Bassett £10,000 and Verrier the rest. Verrier said it was foolproof. I didn't want to go through with it at all but he said I would have to as he was in serious financial trouble."

Verrier forced him to accept the plan as he had information which could ruin Anderson's future. Anderson refused, however, to disappear in Spain and said he would make his own arrangements. He did not sail with the *Christine*. After Bassett had left in her, he and Verrier went to Folkestone where they spent a night at a motel. The following day he flew to Ireland. When he phoned Verrier from there to ask what had happened to Bassett, Verrier replied, "He's like you, Eddie. He's dead."

Anderson said that Verrier would not help him to return to England but offered to get him further afield. Since his return to England he had received constant threats, including an attempt by the driver of a car with false registration plates to force him off the road at sixty miles an hour.

The saga of the *Christine* in relation to the Great Train Robbery had been like a play within a play. For drama and intrigue it almost equaled it, while there was the added complication of a body. But the two proved to be quite unrelated when the true facts of the yacht's disappearance were revealed.

It seems highly probable, however, that the scheme might not have been discovered if there had been no train robbery. The *Christine* had been watched throughout the train robbery investigation by detectives who believed that she might be used to get some of the loot out of the country. Anderson was known to them as a friend of some of the gang.

In the ordinary way there would have been a routine search for the missing yacht and the facts would have been given little newspaper space. But the *Christine* had been linked with the robbery, and her disappearance came under the glare of publicity. Hordes of reporters gave a blow-by-blow account of the search. They sensed that there was more than met the eye in this strange disappearance, which might well have been overlooked. It was a reporter of the *Daily Express*, Brian Park, who flew to Dublin, found Anderson and persuaded him to return to Britain rather than spend his life in fruitless exile.

But the end result of the *Christine* drama added not a tittle of information to the whereabouts of the missing millions.

The bulk of the train robbery money was, in fact, disposed of by a much simpler method than anything yet suggested by crime writers or the police.

During the planning, Johnnie Rainbow devoted almost as much time and energy to this question as to the raid itself. He was thinking in terms not of £2½-million but of a possible £8-million or £9-million haul and he

135

knew that such amounts were too large to be handled through any illegal or unofficial sources. It would need the economy of a whole country to absorb it.

He began a study of the financial set-up of various countries, concentrating on republics which had won a form of independence since the war; countries which were financially sound and strictly ruled, but constantly embarrassed by a shortage of sterling.

There are many such countries in South America, Asia and Africa, and Johnnie had little difficulty in meeting their diplomatic representatives in London. Through an embassy contact from his gambling club days, he was able to get on the invitation lists of the many embassies in the Kensington–Knightsbridge belt where cocktail parties provide a regular meeting place for officials and powerful businessmen from all over the world.

With his easy charm and military manner Johnnie was soon on friendly terms with several members of the Diplomatic Corps. Carefully, he selected his victim, an unconventional patriot who knew more of guerrilla warfare than diplomacy but who talked constantly of his country's need for new British machinery.

At some stage, possibly three months before the robbery, Johnnie sounded out the diplomat. Would his country exchange stock and securities in its various nationalized industries for sterling, with no questions asked about where the money came from? After consultations with his government, the diplomat agreed. It would be an easy, though lengthy, task to get the British banknotes out of the country in the "diplomatic bag," those sacrosanct bundles which go weekly to the parent countries from embassies all over the world with confidential mail, reports and other top secret matters. They often include smuggled luxuries and delicacies which can by no means be classed as "official business." But no country's Customs would ever dream of challenging the contents or asking for these bags to be opened for inspection.

Johnnie then put his plan for the disposal of the money to the gang. After looting the train, he suggested, most of the gang could go straight back to their homes in and around London and, if any questions were later asked about their movements, their wives and families would provide the alibi for them. He and his top lieutenants would take the money in the trucks to the embassy in London. Once the money had passed through the embassy gates, it was on foreign soil and neither the police nor anybody else had the authority—even in the unlikely event that they might eventually trace it there—to do anything about it. As simply as possible he explained how they would each receive yearly dividends from their foreign investments. Should they wish to cash in their capital amounts this would be difficult as it would certainly raise questions by the Bank of England. To do so they would have to live abroad, possibly even change their nationalities, but at least it would ensure crime without punishment—the ideal of every villain.

137

Most of the gang were prepared to go along with Johnnie. His plan appealed to them and they trusted him—at first. Once again the Tippler proved to be the main rebel in the ranks. He was not prepared to trust anyone with his "lolly" and he voiced his sentiments loudly and bluntly. Brian Field, with his knowledge of legal affairs, should have seen the virtue of Johnnie's plan, but with him it was a case of a little knowledge being dangerous.

But the dissension and lack of trust started by the Tippler brought about a new train of events. He was adamant that the money must be counted out in the presence of all the gang so that each would know exactly how much he was entitled to. Arguments that this could take two or more days and that anyway the newspapers would announce the total haul proved useless. In simple terms, he wanted the money in his hands, to burn as he felt fit. He was so involved in the plot that the only alternative to dispensing with his services was to murder him. This was considered by Johnnie and his top echelon but there was no doubt that Tippler's signaling know-how was too important for him to be ditched.

A hide-out where the money could be counted and paid out now became essential. Field soon found a suitable place near the scene of the robbery but sufficiently far away and isolated to be safe for up to two weeks. He organized a purchaser for Leatherslade Farm, supplies and a few diversions such as playing cards, dice and a *Monopoly* set to while away the days of waiting.

138

The counting and share-out of the money took less time than might be imagined. The notes were in bundles of £5,000 and it was a simple matter to multiply the numbers of bundles by this amount. The money destined for the embassy—about £1½-million—was loaded aboard two Landrovers and taken to London by Johnnie and Reynolds on August 9 without incident. They did not dally in the capital but turned round immediately and returned to the farmhouse.

Johnnie advised the entire gang that it was now time to break away. It would be only a matter of time before the police found their hide-out and he and his four principals were leaving that day. Most of the gang decided to stay on a few more days. For some unaccountable reason they felt secure there and, tuned in as they were on short-wave radios to police broadcasts, they were confident that they would get sufficient warning.

Before leaving them to their fate, Johnnie advised them to destroy all fingerprint evidence before they finally broke up. It was agreed that someone should remain for a day after the others left to wash down all polished surfaces and one of the gang—possibly in a mood of self-interest because of his lengthy record—volunteered to do it.

The police announcement which they heard on the radio that the gang was believed to be within a radius of thirty miles of the scene of the robbery was the primary cause of the gang deciding to leave the farmhouse earlier than planned. A lost aircraft which continually circled the area shortly after this announcement panicked them into fleeing. They believed it to be a police spotter plane.

Time was now so precious that their last task was a combined effort to obliterate fingerprints. But once started on this task the heart soon went out of them. Nobody had realized the magnitude of such an undertaking for there wasn't a part of the large farmhouse which they could be sure none of them had touched.

Leatherslade farmhouse would have to be burned to the ground, but if it was done during the day, the fire might soon be noticed and put out. The job must be done at night when firefighters would arrive too late to bring it under control. There was plenty of paint around to ensure that it would burn like a torch.

The gang's next problem was: Where do we go from here? And equally important—how? True, the money had been split up and shared among those who had decided to look after their own spoils, but there was an embarrassing shortage of baggage to stow it in so that it would not be too conspicuous.

Goody remembered that Brian Field, the ambitious solicitor's managing clerk who helped with the legal negotiations over Leatherslade Farm, lived only twenty miles away. His house—which bore the coy but proud sign "Brian and Karin Live Here"—would make an admirable stopping place. They could demand every piece of baggage from them that the Fields possessed and Brian,

140

who must know the area intimately, could navigate them to the safety of his house, outside the search area, on secondary roads where police blocks were not operating. And although Field was not connected with either the robbery or the conspiracy, his part in the negotiations for the farm—in which he covered up for his client—was sufficient to have made him realize by now that, no matter how innocently, he was implicated.

Field's wife, Karin, told the rest of the story in the German publication *Stern* of what happened after the gang panicked.

Mrs. Field said that she and her husband were sitting in their parlor when the telephone rang at 8.00 p.m. She was knitting baby clothes for the child she was expecting in five months' time, while he was reading the latest developments on the train robbery in an evening newspaper.

Field answered the telephone and when he replaced the receiver his face was ashen.

"Who was it?" asked Karin.

In a grim, strained voice her husband answered, "He didn't say. He just said, 'Your friends need you now. Drive immediately to Leatherslade Farm.'"

According to Mrs. Field, she could not understand what was happening but her husband explained about the purchase of Leatherslade Farm, adding, "So, that's what they wanted the farm for. That means I'm right in the thick of the train job now."

141

Mrs. Field counseled him to ring the police but he refused to do so.

"If I do ring the police," he said, "we can say goodbye to our business. You know the kind of people that most of our clients are. There's nothing I can do about it."

Instead of going to the farm as instructed, Field started to drink. By half past eleven, when the doorbell rang, he had got through half a bottle of whisky. Unsteady on his feet, he opened the door to two men who pushed their way past him into the lounge. Mrs. Field described them as smartly dressed in lounge suits, but with a hunted air which caused them to speak in staccato sentences. They told him that Goody wanted to know why he was so long in coming over, and ordered him to get his coat on and go with them to the farm. Mrs. Field saw that her husband was in no fit state to do anything and screamed at them to leave him alone, but one of the men told her, "Sorry, madam, it's too late to bale out now. We need help."

One of the men grabbed her arm and said, "All right, then, you drive."

"That's right," said the other. "Goody said it would be better with a girl. She'd get past the police easier."

When she threatened to give them away to the police on the way, they laughed.

"You'd only land your husband in trouble if you do," she was told. "He fixed the farm for us, remember? Come on—let's go."

While one of the men stayed behind to keep an eye on her husband, she drove with the other in her blue Jaguar to the farmhouse where she was ordered to switch off the headlights.

According to Mrs. Field, the first member of the gang to leave was Roy James. The Weasel ordered her to drive him to Thame Station, where they found that the train service was closed for the night. So he told her to drive him to an address in Bayswater, London, and although they passed several police checkpoints on the way the police waved them through each time.

She arrived back at the farm at 2:00 a.m., to find Gordon Goody waiting for her. He apologized for dragging her into the affair but said it was an emergency.

"Something serious has happened," he told her. "We've heard over the police radio that they're searching every farm within thirty miles of the raid, and we can't stay here. Your house is outside the thirty-mile zone and you've got to help us get there."

When Mrs. Field asked him why he didn't drive to London since the police were not stopping private cars, Goody answered, "We couldn't carry all this money in private cars."

At first Mrs. Field could not grasp his meaning. Then it dawned on her that they wanted to bring the money with them to her house. When she protested that they could never get through to her house with lorries, Goody told her, "That's why we need you—you and this little gadget." He handed her a walkie-talkie radio set and explained that she would lead the two vans. "If there's any trouble," he said, "or if you come to a police checkpoint, send a warning over the radio set."

But this piece of finesse was unnecessary. They didn't see a policeman on the entire journey there.

On arrival at the Fields' house at 3:00 a.m. the gang unloaded the mailbags from the vans and stacked them in the bedrooms, on the landing, in the hall and on the side of the stairs. From Mrs. Field's account it seems that eight of the gang—not counting the man who stayed behind to burn down the farm—were now left of the original team. And among them they had fifty bags of notes. This seems likely to have represented about one-third of the stolen money.

The Fields' nightmarish experience ended two days later after the gang had celebrated their coup with a chicken and champagne dinner during which there was a toast to Scotland Yard. They crammed as many of the notes as they could into the Fields' suitcases, which probably explained why four of his bags containing money were found in the woods near Dorking.

The only man who had spurned the farmhouse as a hideaway was Brian Field, the man who selected Leatherslade and who, as a solicitor's clerk, helped to negotiate the sale. Field had been chosen to find a suitable place because of his intimate knowledge of the area. He lived some fourteen miles from Oakley.

144

His attractive German wife Karen knew nothing about his association with the robbery until the night the gang were panicked by the police announcement.

At the farmhouse the gang discussed ways and means of getting away from the area without being stopped by the police at roadblocks. The only way, they decided, was to get someone who knew all the minor by-roads to guide them, and Field was obviously the man for this. It was the Tippler who telephoned Field at his home with the words: "This is the Leatherslade mob. We need you for another little job and we're coming to get you."

Mrs. Field saw her husband pale and dragged the whole story out of him. Twenty minutes later the gang arrived at Field's house, and told him their plan. When he refused to help them, Tippler grabbed Mrs. Field and warned her husband, "You do as you're told or else your misses is going to lose that baby of hers right here and now on the floor."

Field, not the most courageous of men, slid to the floor, a blubbering mass. But his mentally tougher wife said, "Leave Brian alone. He's finished. I'll get you clear, but no more rough stuff."

She guided them through a succession of country roads away from the area the police were concentrating on and they were able to split up and go their various ways.

The man who stayed behind to burn the farmhouse was jumpy, but the job had its attractions. He was a heavy drinker and there was plenty of liquor in the farmhouse to fortify his courage. By the time evening came he was fairly drunk.

A sudden crackling in the undergrowth at the back of the house set his nerves jangling. He strained his ears and again heard the noise of a snapping twig and dried leaves being trodden on. In the stillness of that late summer night it sounded like a posse of heavy-footed police trackers moving slowly in.

He dropped his matches and fled out of the front door to his car. A hasty look over his shoulder convinced him he was only yards ahead of the Law, for in the bushes he saw a large Alsatian, which he took to be a police dog, sniffing around in a businesslike manner.

In fact the dog must have been from a neighboring farm and was on its nightly sortie after rabbits, or possibly romance.

But for its freak appearance, however, the police who arrived at the farm the next morning would not have had a scrap of the forensic evidence on which they built almost their entire case.

Johnnie and his lieutenants had returned to their homes in London. But when they discovered that the evidence had not been destroyed, all but Johnnie went into hiding. He stayed on at his Mayfair flat, for it was of no concern to him whether his fingerprints were found or not. They had no record of him to compare them with. None of the lesser members who might be caught could identify him by name—even in the unlikely event of

146

their breaking the code and grassing on him. The top members who knew his identity would never in any circumstances give anyone or anything away.

His lieutenants, who all had "form," went into hiding.

Whatever happens to them in the future, their share of the loot is safe. About half of it was still in London by the time the trial ended but by the end of 1964 it will all be out of the country and earning dividends. It has been leaving at the rate of between £30,000 and £40,000 a week.

And there is no chance of its ever being recovered. Even if any of the notes whose numbers are known were identified and traced back to their source from abroad, the British authorities would have to turn a blind eye. They would not risk offending a foreign government over a suspect fiver.

THE RECKONING

9

On the day after a verdict of guilty was returned on eleven of the accused, Fleet Street newspapers held inquests on what had gone wrong with the train robbery plot. Most concluded that there was no master-mind to control the gang after the raid.

"He would have ensured the after-organization of this amazing crime was as thorough as the planning. His discipline would have been stern," declared the crime team of the *Daily Express*.

After outlining how in their opinions the robbery was planned and executed, the *Express* team wrote: "In its execution the Great Train Robbery had been a crime classic. Then came the mistakes. The lack of a mastermind was obvious. There were extraordinary errors arising from panic, gossip. And, contrasting with the finesse shown before, astonishing carelessness. There was panic at the farm four days after the robbery. The gang feared the police net was closing. . . ."

Charles Wilson of the *Daily Mail* came up with the theory that the gang was trapped because the robbery took place a day later than planned. Their original information, he declared, was that the Bank Holiday money from Glasgow would leave there on Tuesday, August 6. When their tip-off man told them the shipment had been delayed a day, the alibis they had worked out collapsed. "There was no Master Mind, no leader to take the decisions," Wilson concluded. "So the men each made their own choice. Some might salvage and rearrange their alibis. But for those like Gordon Goody the 24-hour delay would be fateful. . . ."

In another story the same newspaper also accounted for the disposal of the loot. "Forget stories about midnight sea trips, motor-boats, Swiss banks and helicopters to the Continent," it counseled. "It was all much simpler than that. Two 'chancellors' are arranging the

149

disposal of the cash through betting shops, racecourses and dog tracks.

"Already bookmakers have handled hundreds of thousands of pounds without knowing it came from the robbery. The 'chancellors' back short-price favourites. If they win they get 'straight' money and the bookie's records prove that it is straight. If they lose they just try again with another bookie."

The mass circulation Sunday, *The People*, was the only newspaper which gave credence to Edward Anderson's story that £1-million had sailed with Buster Edwards aboard the *Christine*.

"There is one member of the Great Train Robbery Gang who is smiling this week-end—Ronald Buster Edwards, the man who got away with a cool million pounds," reported Ken Gardner.

"Other men in the gang are either in custody convicted or awaiting sentence, or skulking in hiding in Britain, playing cat and mouse with the police. But Edwards did not go down on the yacht *Christine* when she sank, as was at first thought. He is now believed to have made his getaway to the Continent. Anderson has said that Edwards told him he was to switch to another boat in mid-Channel, and land in France, where a car was waiting to take him to his wife and daughter. But the police theory was that the boat sank with Edwards and the money aboard.

"I can now reveal, however, that Edwards reached

France, where he was to meet other members of the gang on the Continent. For the long-term escape plan was for the gang to make a mass getaway to Latin America. At first the idea was to fly all the key men, plus the loot, in a private aircraft. But the plan was dropped. Instead it was decided that they would all get out of Britain separately and make for South America via the Continent.

"Fake passports and other documents were arranged. International underworld contacts were lined up to change the stolen money. Then they would travel by car through France and Spain in the guise of commercial travellers.

"From Spain across the Straits of Gibraltar to Tangier, where other underworld contacts would fix them sea passages to Latin America. Cuba is believed to have been their final choice of destination. But it was essential to the plan for the raiders to have a breathing space after the raid during which the £2-million banknote loot could be converted through currency fences into jewellery, bonds and other unsuspicious securities.

"That is where the plan misfired. There was no breathing space. The gang panicked at its original hideout in Leatherslade Farm and left hurriedly. Soon the police were hot on their track. And soon arrests were made.

"But Buster Edwards did not fall into the net. With another key man in the gang—and with a major part of the loot—he slipped quietly out of Britain on the *Christine* on the night of January 3. Police are convinced that he did not meet any other members of the gang on the Continent. But he has been able to dispose of a great deal of the loot money through international currency dealers. . . ."

As might have been expected, a man from the *Observer,* Roy Perrott, had been methodically nosing around, sifting and weighing the evidence which he had personally investigated on the spot. He asked, "How does the score sheet look now, eight months after the raid?" and found that none of the four parties concerned—police, criminals, Post Office or the banks—had come out of it "entirely triumphantly."

He reasoned that on balance the police were right to tell the Press they were searching the area within a thirty-mile radius of the robbery.

"Public co-operation was badly needed in covering such a wide area," he wrote. "The police thought it best to flush the raiders from cover; to hustle them into mistakes before they could destroy evidence or conceal their embarrassing two tons of paper. Though it may look obvious now it turned out to be a brilliantly correct hunch by the police."

Perrott faulted the police for their lack of ruthlessness when searching for the robbers. "No helicopters were brought in, for example," he wrote, "though the wanted vehicles at the farm turned out to be plainly visible from the air."

152

In his assessment of where the blame lay, Perrott was most critical of the Post Office who, in the past fifteen years, had suffered several "inconceivable robberies." Yet with three maximum security coaches out of action they had used a coach which was so ancient that its roofing felt was cracked and peeling. There had been no extra guard and many of the mailbags on the floor were not even under padlock. "It is possible," he concluded, "that the next inconceivable robbery is already in the planning stage."

Now let us examine some of the theories and opinions of these experienced crime reporters, at least one of whom had devoted practically all his working hours, from the day of the robbery to the end of the trial, to investigating it.

One wonders how the robbery was executed so neatly if there was no leader, no master-mind, to plan it. Many men were involved, yet during the long months of waiting and briefings not one of them gave a whisper that they were preparing for the biggest criminal coup in history. To any experienced police officer who knows how the informers' grapevine works, this is almost unbelievable, for snouts are strategically placed throughout the underworld—men and women who make a living by informing, who would sell their mothers for the right price. Such silence could have been achieved only by cast-iron discipline and leadership.

Once the job was completed it was every man for himself. No gang leader can dictate to his men what they will do with their money after the pay-out. It is theirs, they have earned it, and he can only advise them about the best channels of disposal. This is what Johnnie Rainbow did, and most of the men went along with his plan.

But Johnnie was not really concerned with what happened to the gang once the robbery had been carried out. He had made his own foolproof arrangements and there was no way the police could connect him with the robbery. He was not known to them and he was confident nobody would squeal.

How right he proved to be! Yet because others blundered after the raid when left to their own devices, it is blandly assumed that they were leaderless throughout the enterprise. From the beginning the police have poured cold water on any talk about a super-planner who might be unknown to them. Naturally enough they wish to give the impression that, even if they cannot prove everything, their knowledge of every aspect of the case is complete.

But with more than £2 million unaccounted for, and three men on their wanted list missing at the time of the end of the main trial, it is obvious that there must be many gaps in their dossier.

It is also difficult to see how such a vast sum of money could be disposed of through betting shops and race tracks. To make any real impression on the money the stakes would have to be huge. As bookmakers' accounts are regularly examined by the authorities, investigations as to where the initial stake money came from would be inevitable.

Nor does it seem likely that the raid was planned to take place twenty-four hours earlier. It needs little knowledge of banking to realize that as Scottish banks are also closed on Bank Holiday Monday, their main collections of English notes spent during the holiday period would take more than a day to sort, total, pack and despatch to London. Johnnie reckoned, quite rightly, that this would take two days, and planned accordingly to raid the train which left Glasgow on the evening of Wednesday, August 7.

The most outright criticism of the way the police handled the case came from Robert Traini on the day after the judge had passed sentence of 307 years on twelve men. Guarded as this crime reporter's remarks were, they contrasted sharply with the almost sycophantic praise heaped on the police by many newspapers and, the next day, by the judge himself.

Traini wrote that now the trial was over, Yard chiefs who control policy and administration stood accused of being fifty years behind the times. "Time and again," he said, "detectives were not allowed to make moves they considered vital. Instead they had to carry out the orders of 'armchair policemen' who, some detectives claim, are out of touch with modern criminal methods.

"The worst administrative errors were in the lack of

155

co-ordination at the Yard and failure to appreciate the value of the right publicity at the right time."

Although he did not name them, he referred to the way the Weasel went on the run because the Yard administrators issued a photograph of him and an appeal for help. The desk men should have known that at *that* moment a team of detectives were on their way to an address where the man was known to be living.

"This error made the man go into hiding elsewhere," wrote Traini. "Months of painstaking work passed before he was interviewed."

He also referred to the way Reynolds escaped a Flying Squad ambush because of a blunder. While praising Detective-Superintendents Fewtrell and McArthur, Triani pointedly omitted any reference to Chief Superintendent Butler, the dedicated, milk-drinking bachelor who, his colleagues had grumbled all along, wanted to make the investigation a one-man show. Readers could only assume that the main target for criticism was Commander Hatherill, who controls Scotland Yard's entire force of detectives from his desk.

Many of the reporters who had worked on the case had similar reservations about police tactics, but the individual policies of their newspapers prevented most from airing them.

Perhaps the most disgraceful feature of the way the case was handled concerns not the police but the department of the Secretary for Air. Fewtrell and McArthur

156

were convinced that the gang were within a radius of thirty miles and thought they could easily find the hide-away with the help of helicopters. Skilled mapreaders would be able to pinpoint the most likely places—remote farmhouses on high land so that the robbers could watch the roads—and these could be immediately investigated. In addition, low-flying helicopters, they reasoned, would panic the gang into fleeing. The police figured that to catch them on the run was safer than trying to over-power them at their hide-out. The latter course might well result in the gang shooting their way past the un-armed police.

At Scotland Yard headquarters the idea was warmly approved of and the Air Department was asked to pro-vide the necessary helicopters. To the astonishment of the police, this was refused. An approach was then made to the American Air Force who told the police they would provide fifty "choppers" with pleasure. As a matter of policy, Scotland Yard was bound to point out that their request to the British authorities had been turned down, so the U.S. authorities decided they had better clear their offer with their British counterparts.

Later that day a senior U.S. Air Force officer made an apologetic phone call to Scotland Yard to say that they were withdrawing their offer of co-operation.

"We can't afford to get mixed up in politics," he added.

Is there anything to prevent another such raid? Ex-

Detective-Superintendent Gosling believes, like Roy Perrott, that the next one is probably in the planning stage. In the hundreds of investigations in which he was concerned over losses from railways, Gosling was never able to establish which body was responsible for the safety of the Mail, either in transit or awaiting collection at railway stations.

The Post Office Police and Railways Police cannot operate away from G.P.O. or Railways property. Conversely, the Civil Police cannot enter Post Office or Railways property unless invited by them to take positive action.

Gosling recalls that when he was in charge of Albany Street C.I.D., two of his men who followed a pair of professional pickpockets into Euston Station were ordered by a Railways Police Sergeant to remove themselves or be arrested for trespassing. So much for liaison.

But since the robbery the Railways have installed radio telephones between mail trains and a central system. This was carried out in the utmost secrecy but it did leak out to a gang which planned a second mail robbery to take place after the Easter holidays. They immediately canceled their plans, thus proving the effectiveness of a simple deterrent which should have been part of the traveling Post Office system for the past thirty years.

Whether the second gang has permanently canceled their plan or merely postponed it while trying to discover how to beat the radio link is not known. If they can regain the odds in their favor there will always be men willing to try to pull a really "big 'un," even at the risk of sacrificing years of precious liberty.

But for the time being, at least, it seems that by a simple stroke of modernization, combined with heavy jail sentences which must act as a deterrent, the authorities have ensured that the mail trains will get through.

THE APPEAL

10

In the two-and-a-half months between the trial sentences and the appeals of the twelve convicted men being heard, there were several interesting developments.

On July third—almost eleven months since disappearing with her husband Bruce—Mrs. Frances Reynolds walked into Cannon Row police station adjoining Scotland Yard and stayed there for several hours. The Yard later issued a statement saying that Mrs. Reynolds was not able to tell them where her husband was.

She had apparently separated from her husband and was anxious to have back her baby son who had been cared for since December by Mrs. Mary Manson, the woman who was acquitted at the preliminary hearing of receiving £835 [$2,338.83] of the stolen mail train money.

But Mrs. Manson had disappeared from her Wimbledon flat with the Reynolds baby. The distraught mother was taken to a secret address by detectives, where, it is believed, she has eventually been united with her son. The search for Reynolds was intensified and there were reports of his being seen in Ireland. Detectives were sent to arrest him, but by the time they got there, there was no trace of him and he was reported to be in Paris.

It seemed obvious to the police that the wives of the two other men still sought might also be getting tired of being away from home and the Yard hoped that in their treatment of Mrs. Reynolds they had illustrated that wives were in no danger of arrest. But the wives of Buster Edwards and James White did not accept these "come into my parlor" advances.

Instead, at least one of the three men still being hunted leaked it to the Law via the underworld, which passed the message to the Press, that he would consider giving himself up and handing over the balance of his cut of the loot if the Appeal Court made drastic reductions in the sentences. The prospect of living out their lives as hunted men had more appeal than being behind bars for between twenty and thirty years.

Meanwhile one of the convicted men who had refused to go along with the master disposal plan of Johnnie Rainbow was bitterly regretting his decision. He had left his share with a trusted friend, but his "friend" was discovered to have left Britain after transferring the £80,000 to Tangier by Gibraltar.

As the train robber was in no position to make an official complaint to the police, some of the underworld friends—shocked to the core at such villainous double-crossing—laid unofficial information. Interpol was alerted but there have been no further developments.

Of more immediate concern to the police were the security arrangements for the appeal. Reports of a daring escape plan with massive outside help were so persistent that it was decided to hear the appeals in batches of no more than three, so that the twelve would not all have to be moved between prison and court at the same time.

A special force of experienced prison security officers was drafted to Brixton Prison to keep a round-the-clock guard on the men while the Law Courts were sealed off by more than fifty policemen.

The appeals to the Court of Criminal Appeal in July, 1964, were heard by Mr. Justice Fenton Atkinson, Mr. Justice Lawton and Mr. Justice Widgery.

The appeals of the first seven men against conviction and sentence were dismissed. But the cases against the

162

two Fields, Brian and Leonard, were considered in a different light.

Both men had been acquitted at the trial of taking part in the robbery but were found guilty of conspiring to rob the train and obstructing the course of justice.

Giving the judgment of the Court, Mr. Justice Fenton Atkinson said that Brian Field had been acquitted at Aylesbury of receiving any of the stolen money even though two bags identified as belonging to him and containing £100,000 were found near Dorking. Field had admitted they belonged to him but claimed they had disappeared from his office.

"There is some evidence to support his evidence that he searched for the bags, and the prosecution did not suggest that he placed them in the wood," said the judge.

Once dissociated from possessing any of the stolen money, the remaining facts against Brian Field were insufficient to enable the jury to infer that he was guilty of conspiracy.

Matter for grave suspicion undoubtedly there was, but having considered the matter as best it could the Court was satisfied that the conviction for conspiracy to rob should not be allowed to stand. His sentence for five years for obstructing the course of justice, however, was not too severe and must stand. It was a grave crime and the convicted men must be punished severely.

Dealing with Leonard Field, the judge said that the prosecution at an early stage of the trial abandoned any suggestion that he was a robber. But it was said he had played an important part in the conspiracy.

It seemed to the Court that those who robbed the train were far more formidable characters than Leonard Field.

"Somebody was required to secure the base but that person need not necessarily be admitted to the inner councils of the conspirators. The evidence strongly suggested that when he went to the farm Leonard Field must have known it was to be used for some criminal purpose. But the jury was not entitled to infer that he knew of the plan to stop and rob the train."

Each man had his sentence reduced by twenty years but the five-year sentences for obstructing justice were unchanged. An appeal by Wheater, the convicted solicitor, against conviction was quashed.

The sentences of Boal and Cordrey, the two men arrested in Bournemouth with £141,000 [$394,941] in their possession, were also slashed. Mr. Arthur James, Q.C., who had prosecuted at the trial, told the Appeal judges that the Crown now felt unhappy over the conviction of Boal as one of the robbers.

Scientific evidence that yellow paint on an article in Boal's pocket was the same paint as that found on a lorry at the gang's headquarters had turned out to be inconclusive.

"Looking back," said Mr. James, "if I had been able to give close attention to it at the trial, I should have invited the jury not to convict Boal of being one of the robbers."

He admitted that Boal's behavior in the dock at the trial after he had been ill might have put the jury against him.

The Court agreed that it might be a miscarriage of justice if Boal's conviction for robbery was allowed to stand and his sentence of twenty-four years was reduced to fourteen years on three counts of receiving.

Six years of Cordrey's twenty-year sentence were lopped off, the view being taken that although he knew the robbery was going to happen, he was not one of the "inner circle" conspirators.

"There are many different shades of guilt according to the part individuals played in it," Mr. Justice Widgery pointed out.

The fact that there were no reductions in the sentences of the seven other men facing thirty years in prison for the train robbery was strongly criticized by the *Daily Herald*.

"They will have to rot in jail far longer than the average murderer," the newspaper's leader writer fumed. "The only justification for sentences of such crushing severity is the need to show that large-scale crime does not pay. It is not an adequate justification.

"Surely it is possible to keep tabs on a released prisoner so that he cannot live in luxury on the loot he has salted away. If the law makes this impossible, the law should be changed."

A comment from another source pointed out that the train robbers had been punished more severely than some of the worst Nazi war criminals.

There were increasing rumors that rather than rot in jail until they were old men, some of the mail bandits— now held in different prisons throughout Britain so that there was not the remotest hope of their once again conspiring together—were offering half of their loot to any gang with the audacity to "spring" them from jail.

As they were all in maximum security jails there seemed little likelihood of any such plan being effective. But the theft of a police van caused the Home Office to instruct prison governors to ensure that gate drill was being strictly carried out. They feared a "Trojan horse" type of escape bid and insisted that only one of the two outside gates at prisons should be opened at a time, while van drivers were checked. Drivers of police vans not recognized by duty wardens now had to remain outside the outer gate while a check call was made to the police authorities concerned.

As a further precaution against escapes, each of the gang was moved every two or three days from cell to cell in different wings of their respective prisons. This should have made it a seemingly impossible task for anyone trying to "spring" them.

But on the morning of August 12, one year and four

days after the great train robbery, the impossible happened. Charles Frederick Wilson, the thirty-two-year-old bookmaker who said not a word in his own defense at the trial, disappeared from his cell in Winston Green Prison, Birmingham.

His escape had the same ingredients as the crime of the century he had taken part in—meticulous planning and audacious execution.

THE GREAT
ESCAPE

It was 3 o'clock in the morning when a gang of three men borrowed a ladder from a builder's yard adjoining Winston Prison and climbed over the fifteen-foot wall. They walked through the jail grounds unchallenged, opened two master locks leading to the maximum security block where Wilson had been placed as a potential escaper and, after coshing patroling-officer William Nichols unconscious, released the train robber.

Wilson quickly changed into some clothes in his cell and by 3:15 he and the others were scaling a rope ladder which the break-in gang had left dangling from the outside wall. A grey Jaguar car was waiting for them and in this they sped down the M1 motorway toward London at 110 miles an hour. By the time the escape was discovered, and the police had put up road blocks on every route out of Birmingham, it was too late. An immediate watch was kept on airfields, ports and on the movements of small boats around Britain's shoreline.

But the man who had received his sentence of 30 years without flinching, and later boasted to his wife, "No jail is ever going to hold me," had disappeared without trace. Some newspaper writers jumped to the conclusion that Wilson was "one of the master-minds" behind the train robbery and that he had been 'sprung' to participate in another big job.

He was, in fact, one of the most minor members of the gang, a crook of limited intelligence whose main asset was brawn rather than brains.

The question now being asked was: how was it possible for Wilson to be released and spirited away from the maximum security cell in the maximum security block of a maximum security prison? Even the Kremlin must have accepted the seeming impossibility of such a task, for the previous occupant of the cell was their master spy Gordon Lonsdale. (Lonsdale, head of an extensive Russian spy ring in Britain, was serving 25 years for espionage. He was exchanged at the Berlin Wall in the

Spring of 1964 for Greville Wynn, a British agent imprisoned in Russia.)

The cell Wilson occupied was specially strengthened and under regular surveillance at 15-minute intervals throughout the night. Duplicates of three keys were necessary to reach it—one for the outside door of the cell block, a second for the steel grille behind the door and a third to open the cell door. At night these doors were double locked with master keys which were kept in a locked safe. This should have ensured that no un-authorized person could get them, while even an author-ized person should not have been able to handle them long enough to get details for the making of duplicates. Nevertheless the gang undoubtedly had duplicate master keys.

The alarm was raised by Patrol Officer Nichols when he regained consciousness and so seriously was the escape regarded that the Home Secretary, Mr. Henry Brooke, was immediately aroused from his bed and informed. He ordered an inquiry and investigators reported to him that the intruders "probably operated in collusion with someone inside the prison."

This at once brought a protest from the Prison Officers' Association whose secretary, Mr. Fred Castell, described the statement as "disgraceful."

"It seems to point the finger of doubt at the prison service," he declared indignantly.

The only light thrown on the affair was by a 43-year-old Salvation Army worker, Mrs. Rose Gredden, who claimed that she had seen three men looking at the prison wall shortly before midnight on the night of the escape. Three hours later when she went downstairs to prepare a bottle for her baby there was a knock on her back door. When Mrs. Gredden called out to ask who was there, a woman's voice asked her the time.

"I told her it was nearly three o'clock," she reported to the police. "I was too scared to go out. But later I looked out of the front window and saw two men in the front of a car and a blond woman wearing a big hat in the back."

At 3:20 she heard two vehicles drive away.

Tips poured in to Scotland Yard that Wilson had been spotted in English coastal resorts, Southern Ireland, France and Italy. Ireland, which waives passport formalities for visiting British, seemed the likeliest bet, for the two countries' mutual extradition treaty had recently lapsed.

His mother, Mrs. Mabel Wilson, was reported to have brushed tears from her eyes when told of his escape and sent him a good-luck message via newspapers "wherever you are, my son."

The Labour Party, eager to seize every opportunity with a General Election only two months away, attempted to make the escape a great political issue with constant demands for the Home Secretary's head. The Party's deputy-leader, Mr. George Brown, declared:

171

"The Home Office has now been the center of so many ghastly mistakes as to make it abundantly clear that administration in that great department must be in an appalling state of confusion and low morale."

Meanwhile the harassed Mr. Brooke was undergoing greater administrative difficulties than his critics imagined. Prison staff uncovered what appeared to be a plot to free Douglas Gordon Goody, the train robber described by Judge Edmund Davies as "a man capable of inspiring the admiration of your fellow accused."

An alert warder noticed that letters to two prisoners at Strangeways Prison, Manchester, where Goody was imprisoned, were in the same handwriting but dispatched from different addresses. Detectives who were called in soon came to the conclusion that it was intended to smuggle in a parcel of money to Goody by way of the other two prisoners. This money was, presumably, to have been used for bribes.

It seems doubtful, however, that Goody was a party to such a plot. He was about to petition the Home Secretary for a re-trial with, it was generally agreed among the legal fraternity, a fair chance of success. His fiancée, Pat Cooper, said she could not believe he would ruin his chances of being legally freed by what she described as "a stupid escape plot."

Her belief in Goody's good sense was reinforced on her next visit to him. He told her that if there was a plan to help him escape, he knew nothing about it. He was

172

confident that he would soon be pardoned on legal grounds and that was the only way he intended to leave prison.

But the Home Secretary released a terse, carefully-worded statement saying, "What appears to have been an outside bid to secure the escape of a prisoner at Manchester was discovered by the prison staff yesterday. The matter was placed in the hands of the police for investigation."

It could have referred only to Goody, as the rest of the men convicted for their parts in the train robbery were scattered in jails throughout the country. In efforts to foil any further breaking-in attempts at these jails to release specific prisoners, the train gang were shuffled about and switched to other prisons. Security was so tightened up, Mrs. Irene Wisbey, one of the wives, complained, that when she was eventually allowed to see her husband who had been transferred to Leeds, he was not allowed to give his infant daughters a cuddle.

For most people Wilson's escape provided yet another thrilling episode in the crime of the century, the repercussions of which seemed endless. It was held generally that the sentences passed on the men had been too savage, so that instead of indignation there was distinct admiration for this latest escapade.

Jack Lucas of the *Daily Herald* pointed out that Wilson was a young man doing 30 years.

"He was in the living death cell," he wrote, "with

nothing to lose, everything to gain. Sentence a man to 30 years and you challenge him to escape. . . . I believe that every long-term prisoner should be given the assurance that his sentence will be reviewed every four years. Even for a train robber there must be something to live for, something to hope for."

The novelist Graham Greene asked in a letter to the *Daily Telegraph*: "Am I one of a minority in feeling admiration for the skill and courage behind the Great Train Robbery? More important, am I in a minority in being shocked by the savagery of the sentences?—30 years for a successful theft as compared with a life sentence (12 years at most in practice) for the rape and murder of a child?

"If our legal system sentences a man to 30 years for an offence against property, it is not surprising if some of us feel sympathy for the prisoner who escapes, again with skill and courage, from such a sentence.

"A great deal is written about prison life in communist countries. Now we learn that in our own out-of-date, overcrowded prisons a man can suffer solitary confinement for an indefinite time, except for a brief period each day when he is distinguished from his fellow-prisoners by a distinctive dress; that he sleeps, if he can, in a cell with an ever-burning light, observed by warders every 15 minutes.

"Is it intended that this treatment should continue over 30 years if the prisoner does not break down and

174

disclose where the money from the Midland and other banks is hidden? This is very close to torture for the purpose of eliciting information—torture on behalf of our banks is even less sympathetic than torture with an ideological motive."

Proof that Greene was not in a minority came the same evening when television interviewers asked people in the streets, "If you knew where Wilson was hiding, would you tell the police?"

There was an almost unanimous "No"—and generally for the same reasons voiced by the novelist.

The criminal fraternity had no such scruples. In jails throughout the country convicts requested interviews with prison governors to pass on scraps of information which might help the police and, incidentally, reduce their own sentences. Such tips caused investigating officers to search the liner Queen Mary and to dash 250 miles to the grim prison fortress at Dartmoor to question a number of prisoners and warders.

In their frenzied efforts to find the missing man the police even adopted the French practice of reconstructing the escape. They placed some credence on a tip that Wilson got out of the search area in a horsebox, traveling as a groom with two thoroughbreds. The horsebox was reported to have traveled westwards along quiet country lanes to a small coastal holiday resort where Wilson boarded a fast launch which took him to Ireland.

One of the senior detectives on the case commented,

"If this was the plan it was a masterpiece. Who would suspect a horsebox traveling through lanes at that time in the morning after the escape? Most policemen would not claim to identify Wilson if he was dressed in riding kit."

Theories flew thick and fast. *The Daily Express* wrote of a master-mind who planned to free the ringleaders of the train robbery for £200,000.

"Key men in the robbery have access to £2,250,000 of hidden loot," the newspaper's crime team wrote. "The second man the gang planned to free, it is said, was Gordon Goody. . . . The third man on the gang's list was Roy (The Weasel) James . . . and the fourth is said to be 31-year-old James Hussey . . ."

On August 20, eight days after his escape, the authorities were convinced that they were closing in on Wilson who was now believed to be aboard a stolen boat, the *Wild Venture.*

The *Wild Venture,* a ketch-rigged 75-ton yacht which had cost its owner, wealthy businessman Mr. Edward Marsh, £80,000, had vanished from its moorings in the Menai Strait off Anglesey the day before. It was fueled and provisioned for a voyage of a thousand miles.

It was spotted by a coastguard off Puffin Island in the Irish Sea and coastguards and police along the entire coastline were alerted. Two Royal Air Force Shakletons of Coastal Command and a Gnat jet fighter scoured the sea while all Navy ships in the area were ordered to keep a sharp lookout. A frigate and a submarine were ordered to leave their base at Clydebank to join the search, and such was the importance placed on the capture of Wilson that Admiral Sir David Gregory, Flag Officer, Scotland and Northern Ireland, personally took charge, plotting the chase like some major war operation.

Wild Venture was sighted only ten miles from Dublin near the search area of the submarine *Olympus*. From his headquarters the admiral signaled, "Intercept and arrest." But the Royal Navy was pipped at the post by British Railways. Before the submarine reached the yacht, it had been arrested by a small railways coaster, the *Sieve More*, which was carrying a cargo of cattle from Ireland to Holyhead in North Wales. The captain of the coaster, George Davey, put his ten toughest seamen aboard the yacht, thinking that there might be strong resistance from Wilson and his associates.

But instead of the train robber they found two seasick teenagers aboard, escapees from one of Britain's borstal institutions where young delinquents are sent for corrective training. Somehow, with no navigational experience, the two boys, aged 16 and 17, had got through the treacherous seven miles of the Menai Straits, a hazard which has claimed hundreds of ships. Two seamen and two officers from the coaster remained aboard to sail the yacht back to Holyhead where the youths were put in prison for the night before appearing before the magistrate.

177

Their escapade had added a further £30,000 to the already astronomical bill the taxpayer was footing for the search for the missing millions and the hunt for some of the key figures behind the great train robbery. And the only new development in almost a year was that, instead of twelve men being under lock and key, now there were only eleven.